A
Borders

Women with Disabilities Working Together

Edited by
Diane Driedger
Irene Feika
Eileen Girón Batres

gynergy
books

Cover illustration by: Mary Montgomery
Cover photographs by: E. Catherine Boldt (1st and 3rd), Irene Feika (2nd)
and Judy Calvin (4th)
Printed and bound in Canada by: Marc Veilleux Imprimeur Inc.

The Council of Canadians with Disabilities is grateful to the Canadian
International Development Agency (CIDA) for financial support for this
book, which does not necessarily reflect the views of CIDA.

gynergy books acknowledges the generous support of the Canada Council.

Published by:
gynergy books
P.O. Box 2023
Charlottetown, PEI
Canada, C1A 7N7

"My Feelings as a Disabled Woman," by Lizzie (Mamvura) Langshaw,
and "The Me the World Doesn't See" and "My Mother," by Shingirai
Pensado, first appeared in *No Application Form: Poems and Stories by Women
with Disabilities From Southern Africa* (International Labour Organization,
1993) and are reprinted with permission. "Life in Trinidad and Tobago,"
by Lorraine Thomas, first appeared in *Trinidad and Tobago DPI Advocate*
and is reprinted with permission. "Begrudging Acceptance: Gender Relations in the Trinidad and Tobago Chapter of Disabled Peoples' International"
was first published in *Creating a Balance: Developing New Relationships Between
Men and Women* (Coady Institute, 1996) and is reprinted with permission.

Canadian Cataloguing in Publication Data

Main entry under title:

Across borders

 ISBN 0-921881-38-X

1. Handicapped women — International cooperation. 2. Women in
development. I. Driedger, Diane Lynn, [date]. II. Feika, Irene.
III. Girón Batres, Eileen.

HV1569.3.W65A27 1996   362.4'082   C96-950011-4

Acknowledgements

We're grateful to have received the encouragement of many people in putting together this book. Thank you to all the contributors for your wonderful contributions and for responding in a timely manner, and over long distances, to tight deadlines. The support of the Council of Canadians with Disabilities (CCD) International Committee, and the help of CCD staff, was integral to our work. We appreciate the assistance of Sibyl Frei and gynergy books on this project. We also thank Beatriz Zeller for her translation of Spanish poems into English.

Contents

Introduction

Women with disabilities are organizing. We have recognized that we face barriers because of sexism and discrimination. We have talents that are ignored and wasted so we have formed our own groups for self-help, to nurture self-esteem and to move forward. Disabled women are uniting in partnerships, and this is happening in every region of the world. Together, we are revealing our talents and moving ahead.

This book is about crossing borders and uniting around a common vision: women with disabilities joined together to demand to participate in society like everyone else. It came about through the international programme of the Council of Canadians with Disabilties (CCD). For ten years, CCD, an organization of people with disabilities, has had partnerships with groups like our own in the Caribbean, Central America, Africa and Asia. In addition to its programming for all people with disabilities, CCD embarked on working specifically with women in 1991. Since then, women have exchanged visits to share information about strategies to enact change, and disability has united us across cultures. We have worked to raise funds for literacy, self-esteem and assertiveness-training programmes, all run by and for disabled women. This book is one fruit of that vision.

Our purpose is to document our experiences of working together and of forming disabled women's self-help groups. Initially, in 1992, CCD put out a call for submissions as part of its "Voice of Women with Disabilities Poetry Project" and we received many poems. We also received poems from the Central American Disabled Women's Functional Literacy project of 1991-95. At first, CCD was going to publish all of these poems as a book. Then, with the encouragement of our publisher, we decided to include essays about disabled women's organizing and put them together with selected poems. We asked women involved in CCD projects to write articles, and added E. Catherine Boldt's interviews with women from around the world at the Fourth World Conference on Women in Beijing, China. These interviews appear throughout the book, as "Snapshots from Beijing."

Across Borders begins with a description of the growth of the disability movement worldwide and goes on to discuss the issues facing women with disabilities in areas such as employment, education, attitudes and violence. We have grouped the essays by region, and have interspersed poetry and snapshots throughout the book. For the most part, accomplished disabled women leaders have written these articles. In one case, an article was written by a non-disabled woman who interviewed women with disabilities. All of the pieces convey the excitement of organizing and the depth of the authors' commitment to a better life for disabled women.

The process of editing *Across Borders* took place over long distances. We editors live in three different cities (Winnipeg, Edmonton and San Salvador) in two countries (Canada and El Salvador). Over the past several years we have written letters, made phone calls and faxed each other. This last year has involved an intense soliciting of articles from all over the world, editing them and communicating with each other as well as with the authors.

We are proud to have edited this book, and, as editors, we reflect a diversity of backgrounds. Diane Driedger has worked in the disability movement locally, nationally and internationally for 16 years. Until four years ago, she was a non-disabled ally of the movement who had an interest in how people organize for change. She has since acquired a back disability. She was involved in the founding of Disabled Peoples' International (DPI), and was CCD's international development officer for more than six years. During that time, she worked closely with women with disabilities in Central America and the Caribbean. Diane is the author of two books and is co-editor of *Imprinting Our Image: An International Anthology by Women with Disabilities* (gynergy books, 1992).

Irene Feika of Edmonton, Alberta has been involved in the disability movement at the provincial, national and international levels for many years. She was chair of CCD from 1986-90, and currently she is the chair of CCD's International Committee. She also serves on the World Executive of Disabled Peoples' International, as the organization's information officer. In this capacity, she is the editor of *Disability International*, DPI's quarterly magazine. Irene has consulted on CCD projects overseas in the last ten years, in the areas of women in leadership, sexuality and disability, and advocacy. She is a woman with hidden disabilities, and is also a mother and grandmother.

Eileen Girón Batres was born in Ahuachapán, El Salvador, which is a small town close to the border with Guatemala. She was one of five children and she contracted polio at the age of one and a half. She went to a regular primary school but could not continue on to high school because the school was inaccessible. As a very young child, Eileen loved to read and she dreamed of being a writer. She studied painting and languages with private tutors.

Eileen became involved in the disability movement in 1979. She is the manager of Asociación Cooperativa del Grupo Independiente Pro Rehabilitación Integral (ACOGIPRI), a Salvadoran organization of disabled persons that operates a ceramics cooperative. She writes more about this in her article in this book. She has served on the regional and world councils of Disabled Peoples' International and has been the editor of the ACOGIPRI newsletter for 16 years.

Through the contributions of its editors and authors, and in its spirit, this book embodies the combined vision of many women with disabilities. What we hope is this: that our work will inform women with disabilities, as well as people in the larger world, about the situation of disabled women, and that it will inspire disabled women to organize and to join hands, like we have, across borders.

Diane Driedger
Irene Feika
Eileen Girón Batres

Diane Driedger

Emerging from the Shadows: Women with Disabilities Organize

Women with disabilities experience discrimination because they are women and because they are disabled. In developing countries, women with disabilities face triple jeopardy: discrimination due to disability, gender and developing world status. Many developing world governments argue that it is difficult to make education, training and employment available to the general population, let alone to disabled people, who have more needs and who are usually seen as non-productive citizens. Disabled persons are thus forced into roles which deviate from the adult social norm — the roles of perpetual child; patient or invalid; curse or blessing from God. Although these roles vary according to disability and culture, they serve to disaffect disabled persons from the rights and privileges of most citizens.

Although women with disabilities have faced discrimination throughout the ages, there has been some positive change since World War II. In wave after wave of social movements, oppressed people have discovered their own histories and challenged injustices. It has been important for marginalized, disadvantaged and colonized people to confront their histories of oppression, to throw off society's view of them as different and society's tendency to decide for them.

THE ROOTS OF THE DISABLED PEOPLES' MOVEMENT[1]

Disabled people have experienced oppression for centuries — they have been locked away in asylums and family attics or considered fit only for domestic work in the family home. In short, they have been shut out of the mainstream of life the world over. However, after World War II, life began to change for people with disabilities.

In the West, improved rehabilitation techniques were developed for injured veterans. People with spinal cord injuries began to live longer. Casualities from other wars increased the ranks of young disabled people and the polio epidemics of the 1950s produced survivors, many of whom were also young people. Improved technical aids such as portable respirators and electric wheelchairs meant that disabled people were much more mobile and able to live independently in the community. In all, there were more disabled young people living more productive lives.

At the same time, the second half of the twentieth century saw the rise of the rehabilitation professions. Doctors, physiotherapists, nurses and social workers were trained to deal with the lives of disabled persons. By classifying them as sick, they tended to medicalize all aspects of life for disabled persons. Because society in general excuses sick people from participating in everyday life, this became another reason to exclude people with disabilities and to deny them responsibility for their lives.

In the 1960s and 1970s, liberation movements swept the developing world. Countries emerged from colonialism in Africa, Asia and the Caribbean. Many people became disabled as a result of liberation and other civil and cross-border wars. Liberation movements in developing countries, and civil rights movements in North America and other parts of the developed world, set the stage for the rise of the disabled people's movement.

ORGANIZATIONS OF DISABLED PERSONS IN NORTH AMERICA

In the early 1970s in the United States, people with disabilities began to organize for their rights. The American Coalition of Citizens with Disabilities (ACCD) was organized nationally in the 1970s but closed down in 1983. Currently, disability groups with many purposes have started up across the country, particularly on the east and west coasts. Today, there are many Independent Living Centres (ILCs) throughout the United States that provide services and individual advocacy.

There are also two large training-oriented groups on the west coast of the United States. World Institute on Disability (WID) works with countries such as Japan, El Salvador and Russia, conducting research and training on international disability issues. Mobility International (MI) USA, which has focused in part on women with disabilities, brings people with disabilities from around the world to Oregon for training in leadership, self-esteem and organizational development. As well, it facilitates exchange trips to other countries for American disabled people. Another group, Disability International (DI) USA, has been organizing since 1992 and has recently become a member of Disabled Peoples' International (DPI).

Not long after the disability movement started in the United States, people began to organize in Canada. Provincial groups were formed in Alberta, Saskatchewan and Manitoba from 1972-74. These were "cross-disability" groups (meaning that they were open to people of various physical and mental disabilities) made up entirely of disabled people speaking for the rights of disabled people, and founded on the premise that uniting people with various disabilities gave them a stronger voice. These provincial groups formed a national organization in 1976 and soon other provinces across Canada became members. This organization was called the Coalition of Provincial Organizations of the Handicapped (COPOH). (In 1994, it changed its name to the Council of Canadians with Disabilities, or CCD, and that is the name I will use for the rest of this article).

DISABLED PEOPLES' INTERNATIONAL

The first international organization to focus on the issues of people with various disabilities was called Rehabilitation International (RI). Composed mostly of non-disabled professionals who work in the areas of disability and disabled persons, it was formed in 1922 and holds a World Congress every four years to discuss matters related to rehabilitation and disabled persons.

In 1980, the World Congress of RI was held in Winnipeg, Manitoba, Canada. At that time, the Swedish delegation brought forward a resolution calling for people with disabilities to have equal representation in the decision-making process within RI. The RI Delegate Assembly turned them down. At the same congress, the Council of Canadians with Disabilities organized after-hours meetings. Several hundred people with disabilities attended each meeting, including about fifty disabled Canadians. (CCD had raised the money for them to attend the congress.) Fired up by the rejection of the Swedish resolution, disabled people decided to form their own international organization composed entirely of disabled people. The mandate of the new organization would be to promote the full participation and equality of people with disabilities all over the world, and to have "a voice of our own."

A steering committee, chaired by Henry Enns of Winnipeg, Canada, was struck to network, plan and fundraise for the founding congress of the new organization. Held in 1981 in Singapore, it included representatives of national disability organizations from around the world. The organization had originally been given the name World Coalition of People with Disablities, but by the time the founding meeting was held, the organization had a new name: Disabled Peoples' International (DPI).

DISABLED WOMEN EXCLUDED

In many countries, women with disabilities were involved in local and national disability organizations and fledgling international organizations. And, like women's experience in other groups and in society, they tended to be in supporting roles or were often given token positions within the executive.

In the early years of forming disability organizations, women with disabilities generally saw themselves as disabled first, and as women second. In Canada, women's issues were not considered serious issues by disabled men in the 1970s and early 1980s. Only when women brought up "important" issues such as transportation, accessibility or housing were they listened to. Few women held leadership positions and they often felt patronized and laughed at.

At the same time as women with disabilities were struggling within disabled persons' organizations in Canada, they found that they also did not feel welcome within the women's movement — they were not seen as "women," only as "different" and "disabled." In general, many women with disabilities did not even identify themselves as "women" because of the attitudes they had absorbed from society and the women's movement.

As the second wave of feminism swept North America and Europe in the 1960s and 1970s, issues important to women with disabilities were clearly not a priority. In addition, many women with disabilities found themselves physically isolated from the women's movement. The chronic underfunding of feminist organizations, coupled with insensitivity to disability issues, has meant and continues to mean that women's events, women's shelters and the offices of women's organizations are inaccessible, that sign language interpretation is not provided, and that hotlines lack Telephone Devices for the Deaf (TDDs).

Women with disabilities, confronted by barriers within disability and feminist groups, decided to organize for their own interests. This has translated into pushing through women's agendas within disability organizations and starting groups specifically for women with disabilities.

CANADIAN WOMEN WITH DISABILITIES ORGANIZE

In Canada, women with disabilities have worked to increase the number of women in leadership positions within the Council of Canadians with Disabilities and to ensure that their issues are addressed by CCD. Thanks to the efforts of a small number of disabled Canadian feminists, the CCD national conference passed a resolution in 1981 calling for equal representation of women in leadership positions and affirmative action policies to make that happen. In 1983, CCD resolved to study women's issues (although

CCD's first discussion paper on disabled women was not published until 1987). In 1985, resolutions were passed that called for a workshop on women's issues at the next conference and for an investigation of women's participation within CCD structure. By the mid- to late 1980s, gender parity was fairly well integrated into CCD. In 1986, Irene Feika was elected as the first female Chair of CCD (a position she held until 1990). Another woman, Francine Arsenault, was the Chair of CCD from 1992-96.

Like the Canadian disabled people's movement ten years before, the disabled women's movement also had its birth in Western Canada. Grassroots women in Saskatchewan held a women's conference in 1984 that eventually led to the formation of the first provincial DisAbled Women's Network (DAWN). Around the same time, a small number of disabled and non-disabled feminists in Manitoba worked together to fight the abuse faced by one disabled woman in that province. Ultimately, they took on other issues facing women with disabilities, calling themselves the Consulting Committee on the Status of Women with Disabilities (CCSWD).

Nineteen eighty-five was an important year in Canadian disabled women's organizing. Women with disabilities organized a "Women with Disabilities Networking Meeting" in June. It was attended by delegates from across Canada. A steering committee was struck to set up a national organization called DisAbled Women's Network (DAWN) Canada. Delegates agreed to return home and start their own groups of disabled women. That year, local groups were founded in Toronto, Montreal and Ottawa, and provincial groups formed in Prince Edward Island and Nova Scotia. British Columbia founded its group in 1986. In March 1987, the founding national meeting of DAWN Canada was held in Winnipeg.

Since then, DAWN Canada has researched the concerns of disabled women and has published position papers on issues such as self-image, employment, parenting and violence. These issues — especially violence against women with disabilities — have been traditionally overlooked by both the women's and the disabled persons' movements.

In recent years, DAWN Canada has worked with both women's organizations and the disabled people's movement. As a result, Canada's largest feminist organization, the National Action Committee on the Status of Women (NAC), now holds its meetings in accessible locations, has an accessible office and actively looks for ways to support its disabled sisters around the country.

DAWN Canada has also joined with CCD to work together on issues of broad social policy and has worked with another group of disabled persons, the Canadian Disability Rights Council (CDRC), to make sure that disabled women's rights are protected under the Charter of Rights and Freedoms. (This is a part of the Canadian constitution that prohibits discrimination on many grounds, including disability.) Recently, DAWN and CDRC have published a series of papers on the implications of new reproductive technologies for women and disabled persons.

Despite this progress, the women's and disabled persons' communities in Canada still need to do more work to ensure recognition of the importance of disabled women's issues. And the same struggle is faced by women with disabilities around the globe.

DISABLED WOMEN IN OTHER COUNTRIES

While organizations of disabled persons have sprung up in over 100 countries since 1945, women have been poorly represented — or not represented at all — in decision-making positions. As in Canada, women's issues have not been seen as important by the greater disabled persons' or women's movements. At the national level, very few separate disabled women's organizations exist. At present, women have formed their own groups only in Australia, Canada and Uganda and are working on becoming a separate group in Trinidad and Tobago.

In Australia, women with disabilities have been very active within the disability movement for years. They formed their own organization in 1995 — it is separate from the greater disabled persons' group, but still retains membership in that group. Women with Disabilities Australia (WDA) has a newsletter and funding from the Australian government for its office.

The Disabled Women's Network of Trinidad & Tobago (DAWN T&T) was formed in 1992 and, since then, has held numerous training workshops on self-esteem, educational enhancement and health maintenance. Violence and employment are issues that DAWN T&T intends to focus on in the coming years. (See my article with Kathleen Guy, on page 71 for more information about DAWN T&T.)

The Uganda Disabled Women's Association (UDWA), formed around 1986, is also involved in self-help. In support of its goal to contribute to the well-being of disabled women in Uganda, the group operates a craft store to sell its own products and has managed its own revolving loan fund since 1991. The group is proud to state that "... many who were beggars are no longer so and are thus contributing to national development. Incomes received from this form of employment breathe life into the ... beneficiaries by improving their standards of living and rendering them more responsible and self-supporting."[2]

Disabled women have also addressed underrepresentation in the disabled persons' movement by forming caucuses within those organizations. Although traditional views regarding women have made gains difficult, the caucuses provide disabled women with the opportunity to formulate their own ideas first and then present them to the greater membership for action. There are women's caucuses in organizations in countries such as: Cambodia, Costa Rica, Dominica, El Salvador, Jamaica, Malaysia, Mauritius, South Africa, St. Lucia and Zimbabwe.

WOMEN WITH DISABILITIES IN DPI

Within Disabled Peoples' International (DPI), women with disabilities have spoken up and pointed out that very few women are leaders in local, national or international organizations. At the 1983 DPI World Council Meeting, a resolution calling for more representation for women was not acted upon. In 1984 in Jamaica, women with disabilities met separately at a DPI symposium on development and again asked for equal representation. Again, no action was taken.

Nineteen eighty-five became a watershed year for women with disabilities within DPI. At the DPI World Congress in the Bahamas that year, DAWN Canada organized three meetings for women with disabilities. Strong leadership from the Australian delegation, Dr. Fatima Shah of Pakistan and DAWN Canada, along with lots of hard work, led to the presentation of a resolution at the main DPI meeting that called for fifty percent representation by women in decision-making. The resolution passed.

Since then, DPI has created a Women's Committee with representation from all the regions. DPI has held leadership training seminars for disabled women in different parts of the world and, in

1985, created a Deputy Chair position to look at the inclusion of underrepresented groups in DPI — including women, deaf persons and people with mental disabilities.

Although the representation of women in DPI has increased at all levels since 1985, there is still much progress needed before equality can be reached. DPI's World Council is about one-third women. Of DPI's five Regional Councils, only two have equal representation for women and men: Africa and the North American & Caribbean Region. In the other three regions (Latin America, Asia/Pacific and Europe), the representation for women is thirty percent or lower.

INTERNATIONAL NETWORKS OF WOMEN WITH DISABILITIES

Several international disabled women's networks have formed in the last decade. In 1985, even as women were challenging DPI to include disabled women in decision-making, women with disabilities were mobilizing on their own.

Like the conference in Beijing ten years later, the World Conference to Review the Achievements of the United Nations Decade for Women, held in Nairobi, Kenya, in July 1985, was inaccessible. At a workshop about barriers to women with disabilities, disabled women from fourteen countries decided to form their own organization, called Disabled Women's International (DWI). The final report from the Nairobi conference called on governments to provide opportunities for disabled women to participate in all aspects of life.

The intention behind the formation of DWI was to facilitate information sharing among women with disabilities in different countries. Delegates to the Nairobi conference went home and encouraged others to join. DWI published one information-sharing newsletter annually for the first few years, but, due to a lack of funding, little else has been accomplished.

Partially as a result of DWI's inaction, and because no DWI women attended the August 1990 United Nations Meeting of Disabled Women in Vienna, the World Coalition of Women with Disabilities (WCWD) was founded. WCWD's mandate was to advocate for the concerns of disabled women in the disabled and women's movements. DAWN Canada, chaired by Pat Israel at that time, was the driving force behind WCWD and, in 1992, organized a WCWD meeting of disabled women to coincide with a disability conference called Independence '92. Since then, however, DAWN Canada's leadership has focused on national issues and WCWD is no longer an active organization.

In September 1995, one day prior to the Fourth World Conference on Women in Beijing, China, an International Symposium on Women with Disabilities was held at the conference site. The symposium was organized by Disabled Peoples' International, the World Blind Union, Mobility International USA and the World Federation of the Deaf. Over two hundred women with disabilities attended. Although woefully inaccessible (as described in detail in E. Catherine Boldt's article on page 150), the symposium and the Fourth World Conference on Women provided a tremendous opportunity for women with disabilities to network and to flex political muscles in the international media.

Although women with disabilities know that they have a long way to go before they will truly have equality of opportunity comparable to that of non-disabled persons, they are beginning to enjoy the fruits of their efforts the world over.

ISSUES FACING WOMEN WITH DISABILITIES

Worldwide, women with disabilities are emerging from the shadows to establish women's caucuses, self-help organizations and income-generating ventures. Nonetheless, poverty and limited opportunities continue to define their status around the world. As women with disabilities organize, they must confront the problems of access, housing and transportation that are faced by every disabled person. These barriers, coupled with the unique challenges faced by women with disabilities — negative attitudes, lack of role models, lack of education and many forms of violence — prevent them from taking their rightful place in society.

WOMEN WITH NO PLACE IN SOCIETY

By and large, women with disabilities lack the opportunities to fill positive societal roles. The image of a disabled woman does not flash to mind when words like colleague, doctor, engineer, wife, mother, friend are spoken. Given that there are few positive role models for women with disabilities, they are left to feel invisible and without goals. Myths about disability lead to profound social, political and economic consequences for women.

Attitudes form a huge barrier to the education and employment of people with disabilities. There is a widespread perception that if you have some sort of physical disability, you cannot think or work. People who are mentally handicapped face the perception that they cannot learn or work at all. The prevailing attitude is that disabled persons are recipients, not contributors.

These attitudes are magnified towards women with disabilties. Prejudices regarding the competency of women and their ability to measure up to men exist to varying degrees in countries around the world. Women with disabilities are often overprotected in the home and their families do not view their education as a priority. On the other hand, some families in the developing world see women with disabilties as houseworkers and want to keep them at home.

The lack of role models and negative attitudes about disability have the greatest consequences for women in developing countries. The roles of wife and mother are often the most important roles assigned to women — they give women societal status. If a woman is unable to participate in this role, she is seen as a non-person.

To quote Dr. Fatima Shah, a blind leader from Pakistan, "... always conscious of her lack of a place in the social order, she [the blind woman] is gradually brainwashed into accepting herself as a non-person with no rights or privileges to claim, no duties or functions to perform, no aim in life to achieve, no aptitudes to consult or fulfill."[3]

THE STRUGGLE FOR EDUCATION AND EMPLOYMENT

The vast majority of the world's 500 million disabled people are illiterate, and disabled women are less likely to be literate than disabled men. Most of the 350 million disabled people living in developing countries have no formal education.[4]

To begin with, physical barriers to transporation and schools prevent disabled children from getting an education. Moreover, the attitudes of families who want to keep their disabled daughters at home to do chores inhibit disabled women's education. In those developing countries where there are opportunities for basic education or training, disabled boys — not girls — usually receive them. Zohra Rajah, a mobility impaired leader from Mauritius and formerly a Deputy Chair of DPI, has remarked, "In many societies it is difficult to convince people that able-bodied women need to be educated; for disabled women it is worse. Due to traditional role perceptions, disabled women are given less encouragement to continue with education."[5]

In developed countries, education is often affordable and more women are literate, but people who are disabled still face barriers to access and success in publicly funded schools. Governments and communities are slow to remove the barriers which impede disabled peoples' success in the education system.

There is a general lack of support and encouragement for women with disabilities in every sphere of life, and nowhere is this more blatant than in the workforce and opportunities for training. In some developing countries, the traditional training of both women and men with disabilities tends to over-emphasize the acquisition of the simplest craft skills, regardless of the individual's educational level or interest. There is nothing wrong with training in craft skills, but disabled people want the opportunity to follow their vocational interests and to have access to the highest paying jobs.

Systemic barriers in society also present significant obstacles to securing employment. These barriers include inaccessible public transportation, offices with stairs, office equipment at the wrong height and lack of TDDs. Job positions which require ongoing expenses, such as sign languange interpretation for a deaf employee, are even harder to obtain.

Finding employment is among the greatest challenges for disabled women globally. Those who find employment are often ghettoized in the lowest paying jobs — for instance, they may work as street vendors selling fruit or administrative clerks. Because disabled people have difficulty finding employment, many disabled persons' organizations in the developing world are starting their own businesses. In Soweto, South Africa, disabled people started the Self-Help Factory, which specializes in electronics, because it was impossible to get accessible transportation to mainstream employment. In Trinidad and Tobago, the Disabled Women's Network is starting several businesses and training its members for the jobs.

VIOLENCE AGAINST DISABLED WOMEN

Many disabled women live in situations characterized by a high degree of economic and social dependency, whether they live with relatives or in an institutional setting where services are provided by paid caregivers. Unfortunately, their lack of power leaves them more vulnerable than usual to violence.

Common forms of abuse encountered by women with disabilities can include: "... criminal acts such as assault and sexual assault or negligence (not washing, feeding or toileting an individual); human rights violations (such as sexual harassment); verbal taunting; degrading, humiliating behavior; rough handling; or isolation through silence. Abuse can take place once, or it can happen on an on-going basis."[6]

Some disabled women require assistance with many of the activities of daily living. Because more people have access to the intimate aspects of their daily lives, either in their familial homes or in the institutions where they reside, these women are more vulnerable to assault. Considering the isolation and anonymity of women with disabilities in the community, the potential for both emotional and physical abuse is high. It has been estimated that having a disability doubles an individual's likelihood of being assaulted.

Few statistics exist to substantiate the issue of abuse of women with disabilities in developing countries, but Canadian figures speak boldly about the magnitude of the violence. In a 1989 survey of women with disabilities, 40 percent of the women had been raped, abused, or assaulted; 64 percent had been verbally abused. Girls with disabilities have even less chance of escaping violence. Women with multiple disabilities are multiply abused,[7] and moreover, women with disabilities have little access to services for victims of violence. There is little to indicate that the situation for women with disabilities has changed in Canada since 1989, or is any better in developing countries.

Consider the circumstances: Disabled women are often trapped in the home with their abusers, and women's crisis services tend to be both attitudinally and architecturally inaccessible. In many developing countries, there are no shelters for battered women at all. Women with disabilities are also likely to have fewer people to turn to for help and fewer resources to create services to help escape or recover from violence.

While disabled women in developed and developing countries confront abuse daily, this problem has received scant attention from policy makers and service providers, despite pressure to confront the problem from disabled feminists in developed countries.

SEEN AS NON-SEXUAL

Because society often views women with disabilities as asexual, many do not receive appropriate sex education from their parents. It is assumed that disabled women will not attract men because they are undesirable. Disabled survivors of assault report that no one believed that they had been assaulted. The typical response to their claims was a callous, "Who would want to rape a disabled woman?"

Women with disabilities are also discouraged from marrying by their families and communities. In some countries, families reinforce society's view of disabled persons as undesirable by hiding disabled girls in their homes. They believe that having a disabled family member could ruin the marriage opportunities for the whole family.

Women everywhere feel pressure to conform to the perfect body-beautiful images with which they are bombarded. Those pressures are magnified for women with disabilities. As a result, women with disabilities experience low self-esteem and a sense that they are unattractive. Society's image of disability, and the woman's own ideas about her body, lead to a self-defeating circle of misconceptions. The consequences of this mythology are devastating. Lack of information has resulted in sexual abuse — sometimes because the woman doesn't know she has the right to say "no" — unwanted pregnancies and sexually transmitted diseases. The concerns of women with disabilities are ignored when services are created to improve sex education and reproductive health, provide child care and offer services such as rape crisis centres.

VIOLENCE IN OUR COMMUNITIES

Societies the world over do not value women, and they especially do not value women with disabilities. This has led to a range of violent acts against women. In many developing countries, women with disabilities are harassed when they appear in public. This harassment can vary from name-calling to physical attack. Many women with disabilities have been considered to be outcasts because their disability cannot be cured, or have been treated as specimens in teaching hospitals. The message in many cultures is clear: Disabled women should not be visible — in the street, in jobs around their communities or even in their homes.

During times of war, the obstacles to survival are greatly increased for people with disabilities. Disabled people are often left behind when their fellow citizens are fleeing war zones. Disabled refugees are not always welcome. Because women are often considered the spoils of war and subjected to rape and other degradations, women with disabilities are even more vulnerable to this kind of assault.

Finally, genital mutilation — or female circumcision, as it is sometimes called — affects some 75 million women. While the highest incidence of genital mutilation occurs in Africa and the Middle East, cases have been reported in Australia, Brazil, Pakistan, England and Russia. These practices are sanctioned by a variety of religions using a range of justifications such as encouraging cleanliness, preventing promiscuity, ensuring female virginity at marriage and preventing women from finding sex pleasurable. These procedures often have a disabling affect upon women, resulting in physical illness and permanent physical or mental disability.

Genital mutilation has much in common with many other forms of women's oppression. Like the involuntary sterilization of mentally disabled women, which still occurs in parts of the developed world, genital mutilation is an example of how little control women exercise over their own bodies.

CONCLUSION

Globally, women with disabilities are continuing to organize to promote improvements in their economic and social status. They have worked within the disability movement and the women's movement to demand room for themselves and their issues. They have started their own groups and committees in order to focus on their own concerns.

Today, they are much more aware of the extra barriers faced by women with disabilities. They are working at the community level to make a difference for women. In many countries, disabled women are coming together for the first time to discuss problems and to strategize for change. They are working with the disability movement and women's organizations to remove the barriers to their full participation in society. Around the world, they are making connections, working together, learning from each other and supporting each other in their efforts to take their place within their societies and communities and homes — a place where women with disabilities have as many choices and opportunities as everyone else.

NOTES

1. The historical information provided in this article is based on research presented in: Driedger, Diane, "Discovering Disabled Women's History," in *The More We Get Together: Women and Disability*, Houston Stewart, Beth Percival and Elizabeth R. Epperley (eds.), (Charlottetown, Canada: gynergy books, 1992), pp. 81-93. Some of this research was also published in: *Resources for Feminist Research/Documentation sur la recherche féministe* (Vol. 20, Nos. 1&2, Spring/Summer 1991); and, with April D'Aubin, in *Canadian Women's Studies* (Vol. 12, No. 1, Fall 1991); *Match News* (Spring 1991); *Women's Education des femmes* (Vol. 8, No. 3/4, Winter 1991); and *Healthsharing* (Winter/Spring 1992).

2. *Uganda Disabled Women's Association Newsletter*, Jan/Feb 1995, p. 7.

3. Shah, Dr. Fatima, "The Blind Woman and Her Family and Participation in the Community (Rural)," in *Women, Development and Disability*, Ann Gajerski-Cauley (ed.), (Winnipeg, Canada: Coalition of Provincial Organizations of the Handicapped, 1989), p. 20.

4. Fricke, Yutta, "International Year for Literacy: Education for All?" *Vox Nostra* 1 (1990), pp. 6-7.

5. Rajah, Zohra, "Thoughts on Women and Disability," *Vox Nostra* 2 (1989), p. 10.

6. McPherson, Cathy, *Responding to the Abuse of People with Disabilities*, (Toronto, Canada: Advocacy Resource Centre for the Handicapped, 1990), p. 1.

7. Ridington, Jillian, *Beating the "Odds": Violence and Women with Disabilities*, (Vancouver, Canada: DAWN Canada, 1989), p. 1.

Monica Bartley

Women First, Disability Afterwards: The Combined Disabilities Association Women's Group

WOMEN AND DISABILITY IN JAMAICA

Many Jamaican women are the sole breadwinners in their families. They are thus responsible for housing and feeding their children, maintaining family living standards and ensuring that children are cared for while they work outside the home. Jamaican women are also active in most sectors of the economy. They have demonstrated their skills and resourcefulness in industry, trades, services, agriculture and the public sector.

Even though real power still lies in the hands of men, disabled women in Jamaica could not conceive of the need for the liberation of women in a society where, for many years, women have played quite a dominant role in managing their own affairs and holding a place in the job market. At the forefront of their minds, the real struggle is for the recognition of the rights of persons with disabilities.

Disabled persons in Jamaica face issues such as poverty, high unemployment, and a lack of education and training opportunities — all of which have subjected them to a life of charity. They have often experienced years of neglect of their abilities and abuse of their rights. As a result of society's attitude towards them, many disabled persons have low self-esteem and are lacking in self-confidence. They are also unable to participate fully in society because of physical barriers: inaccessible buildings, which are not designed to accommodate wheelchairs; a public transportation system which is inaccessible while private transportation is unaffordable to most; and a lack of affordable and accessible housing.

HISTORY OF THE CDA WOMEN'S GROUP

The Combined Disabilities Association (CDA) of Jamaica had its origin in the Citizens Committee for Progress of the Handicapped (CCPH), which had its first meeting in December 1976. CCPH was established through a resolution adopted on New Trends in Mental Retardation, which called for a watch-dog committee on "Law and the Handicapped." In spite of the impact of that work, it was soon recognized that the watch-dog committee of CCPH needed to expand its role into a full-fledged organization of disabled persons.

In 1979, discussions between persons with different types of disabilities led to the formation of a multi-disability steering committee. This steering committee, led by Huntley Forrester, became the Combined Disabilities Association (CDA). On June 6, 1981, approximately 60 disabled persons launched the CDA by adopting a constitution and electing a Board of Directors consisting of ten persons—seven men and three women.

Prior to the formation of the CDA Women's Group, there existed a group of physically disabled women called the Mona Rehabilitation Old Girls Association (MROGA). MOGRA had formed in 1976 and the women of MROGA shared the common experience of living at the Mona Rehabilitation Centre. This group acted in a social welfare capacity, by counselling physically disabled girls and women living at the Centre, as well as those who lived at home and needed help. It provided role models for the girls living at the Centre and financial assistance for those who were no longer living there, and also helped women to find employment.

Although formal meetings are no longer held, MROGA is still active through networking. Approximately five physically disabled women in the group respond to the various needs of other physically disabled girls or women. MOGRA women, including myself, are also members of the CDA Women's Group, where we act as resource persons.

The Women's Group of the Combined Disabilities Association evolved from the CDA following the Disabled Peoples' International World Assembly, which was held in Jamaica in 1984. There, a group of disabled women was addressed by Dr. Fatima Shah, who sensitized us to issues facing disabled women internationally. This spurred us to establish a group of our own. Among the women in attendance at the assembly were some of the core members (Valerie Spence, Sarah Newland and myself) of the MROGA, and we had little difficulty with the idea of expanding our group into a cross-disability women's group.

From 1984 to 1987, the women's movement in Jamaica was gaining momentum. Initially, it was very difficult for the women's movement to attract the interest of a wide cross-section of disabled women because the disability rights movement was just starting to gain momentum in Jamaica. It became difficult to focus on specific women's issues within the disability rights movement.

In 1987, however, a few disabled women got together and decided to form the Combined Disabilities Association (CDA) Women's Group. We recognized the need for disabled women's voices to be heard, were determined to see it happen and decided to press on. For guidance, the group (which included Sarah Newland, Valerie Spence, Eloise Rhone and myself) met with Linette Vassell, an advocate of the Jamaica women's movement. She helped us identify the problems we faced and gave advice on how to get the group started. She encouraged the group to hold regular meetings, even if there were only a few persons in attendance. After this, about six of us women met on an ad hoc basis.

In 1988, the Disabled Peoples' International North American & Caribbean Region Women and Development Seminar was held in Dominica. The focus of this seminar was to teach leadership skills to women with disabilities and to unearth their leadership potential, as well as increase their self-esteem and develop their parenting skills. This seminar was a success — it became a turning point in the disabled women's movement in Jamaica. The women who attended were further sensitized to disability issues and were encouraged to advance their cause. One woman, Delcie Pascoe, reported that, at this seminar, she discovered her true potential and returned home highly motivated to lead the women's group. The sharing of experiences gained at this workshop was a source of inspiration to disabled women locally. It helped to rid quite a few women of their reticence and enabled them to enter into the mainstream of society.

Regional seminars, which are training sessions conducted by the DPI North America & Caribbean Region every two years, have also provided exposure for the women and allowed discussion of topics, such as the sexuality of disabled persons, which were prevously not openly discussed. In Jamaica, very little information is passed on to disabled women about sexuality or sexual reproduction and the potential impact on a woman's disability. Consequently, some women have experienced serious emotional trauma when they are unable to have a full term pregnancy or their baby does not survive. Jamaica's most memorable regional seminar was held in 1987, when Irene Feika presented the video Choices, and the topic of sexuality was discussed openly with a cross-disability group of men and women. This helped many disabled persons to see themselves as sexual beings.

Following the 1988 Women in Development seminar, more women were motivated to become involved with the CDA Women's Group and, in 1989, under the leadership of Delcie Pasco, membership increased to approximately 30 persons, with 15 to 20 in regular attendance at meetings.

I continue to work very closely with the coordinator of the CDA Women's Group in planning activities, and, as the person within CDA responsible for training, I secure resource persons to conduct sessions with the group. One such session covered the topics of peer counselling and building a positive self-image, and included presentations by two disabled women with whom the group could easily identify.

EXPECTATIONS OF THE CDA WOMEN'S GROUP

The expectations of the group are many and varied:

1. Economic;
2. Education;

3. Advocacy;
4. Fellowship; and
5. Collaboration.

The group has the following aims and objectives:

1. To develop self-confidence, self-esteem, self-reliance and a high level of assertiveness;
2. To deal with problems that are peculiar to women;
3. To assist unskilled/unemployed disabled women in acquiring skills and to prepare them for employment and self-employment.

Our motto is: "Women first, disability afterwards."

ISSUES FACING THE WOMEN'S GROUP

The Combined Disabilities Association Women's Group is a multi-disability group drawn from the membership of CDA. It includes women who are blind, physically disabled, hearing impaired and mentally handicapped. Most of the women are unskilled, unemployed, experience low self-esteem and lack self-confidence. The educational level of women in the group ranges from primary to tertiary (tertiary refers to post-secondary education). The majority of the women, however, have only primary education and are in need of some form of training or vocational skills to enable them to obtain employment. There is a critical need for these persons to upgrade themselves, but this usually cannot be done because of the lack of training sponsorships for persons with disabilities. However, where someone can fit into a skills-training programme, she is referred and we have tried to address some problems by inviting resource persons to speak about ways in which one can become self-employed.

Inaccessible transportation, the cost of bus fares and the difficulty of finding a suitable venue makes it hard for people to attend meetings. The membership is seeking solutions for these issues. As long as we lack a suitable meeting place or accessible office space we cannot develop a firm foundation and some of our programmes cannot be implemented.

Funding is also crucial to the long-term viability of the group; otherwise, we are very limited in the programmes we are able to implement. The group has made applications to both local and international funders and recently received a positive response from MAMA CASH (based in Amsterdam, Netherlands) for a series of workshops on gender issues as they relate to disabled women. The programme of the group is designed to address some of these issues.

THE WOMEN'S GROUP AND NETWORKING

In the early stages of the group's existence, networking was a very strong part of our activities. We disabled women were well received by other women's groups and, as a result, invitations were extended to us from various women's groups to attend meetings, seminars and workshops on women's issues. This provided us with exposure and sensitized us to matters affecting women nationally and internationally, as well as giving us the opportunity to air our issues to a wider public. Chief among these groups was the Bureau of Women's Affairs (a government organization) which held monthly round table discussions on issues such as violence against women and women's health.

Sistren, a group of grassroots women who use drama to portray issues affecting women, is another organization which invited the involvement and participation of the CDA Women's Group in their formal presentations as well as their social functions. In return, the CDA Women's Group invited Sistren to do an exposition portraying disability issues at one of our monthly meetings.

The Women's Media Watch, an organization which monitors the images of women in the media, also invites disabled women to participate in their activities. We have been invited to view and critique movies on issues such as sexual harassment, violence against women and negative media images of women. In fact, a physically disabled woman, Evelyn Scott, is now employed by this organization and is included as a member of the Media Watch team in their public presentations. She represented them at the recent International Women's Conference in Beijing, China.

The CDA Women's Group has benefited significantly as a result of our membership in the Association of Women's Organizations of Jamaica (AWOJA). They ensure that all draft national legislation pertaining to women is reviewed by the CDA Women's Group. We have formed part of AWOJA's official delegations, which also include representatives from other women's groups such as Women's Media

Watch and Sistren. These delegations have met with Ministers of Government to discuss issues of importance to women. As well, a disabled woman is employed as AWOJA's administrator.

Women with disabilities have been exposed to gender issues through their involvement with other women's organizations and through sponsorships to attend a three-month workshop on gender studies in Barbados and to participate in ongoing one-year courses at the University of the West Indies. In 1994, two disabled women received sponsorships — one for the Barbadian workshop and one for the University of the West Indies course.

The effect of this type of involvement is twofold. It fosters the process of integration and acceptance of disabled women by other women. Having been made aware of the disability issues, these women help in finding solutions. The exposure has borne fruit, in that disabled women have become more vocal on issues related to women. Some of these women also became members of other women's groups, such as Women's Media Watch, Women's Resource Outreach Centre and the Caribbean Association for Feminist Research and Action (CAFRA). Their involvement included playing leading roles in these organizations — serving on the boards and representing the organizations nationally and internationally.

Another very positive event which had an impact on the development of disabled women's groups in Jamaica was the establishment of a linkage with disabled persons in Kingston, Ontario, Canada. Initially the linkage was established with CDA, as a channel for an interchange of ideas and as a way to get wheelchairs and crutches for persons who were unable to afford them. Later, the focus shifted to the Women's Group of CDA.

The linkage got started through discussions with Tony Wong (a past Executive Director of CDA), Huntley Forrester, and Jean Moore (a Canadian who visited Jamaica in the 1980s). This occurred at a time when linkages were taking place in the wider society. Canadian University Services Overseas (CUSO) was approached to fund the linkage with a group of disabled persons in Kingston, Ontario. Initially the linkage took the form of an exchange of persons — Derrick Palmer and Tony Wong visited Canada and conducted workshops. This resulted in a further collaboration with Queen's University and Mona School of Physiotherapy which, along with DPI North American & Caribbean Region, conducted a survey on public knowledge of, and attitudes towards, persons with physical disabilities. CDA also benefited from the visits of Canadians such as Francine Arsenault and Irene Feika, who shared experiences and conducted workshops with Jamaican disability groups.

As part of the linkage, two women from the CDA Women's Group visited the Council of Canadians with Disabilities (CCD) in Canada and benefited from the exposure they received to new ideas, new technology and cultural interaction with the Canadians. This interaction brought into sharp focus the reality that living with a disability in Canada was much easier than living with a disability in Jamaica. In Canada, various assistive devices are available and people have the ability to network widely and communicate quickly via the computer. One of the Jamaican women was particularly impressed with the speed with which information was disseminated, which allowed for much more to be achieved in a timely manner. As well, the knowledge that there were persons with disabilities elsewhere living independent lives despite the severity of their disabilities strengthened the solidarity and the determination of the Jamaican women to continue the struggle. These experiences were shared locally and the networking between the two groups has become a motivating factor for us.

Our group has suffered from periods of inactivity. This inactivity has been due mainly to the lack of leadership skills among the women. The most recent lull in our activities was from 1991-94. During each of these periods, however, efforts have been made to reactivate the group. The women from the group have continued to participate in the activities of women's groups nationally. The Combined Disabilities Association Women's Group, as a member of the umbrella organization AWOJA, is kept abreast of national events and provides input so that the voices of women with disabilities can be included in all issues of national importance.

HOW WE HAVE CHANGED GENDER RELATIONS IN CDA AND JAMAICA

Since 1989, there have been more women in leadership positions within CDA, a reversal of the previous situation, where the board was predominantly male. For example, in 1981, when CDA was formed, the top leadership positions — those of Chairperson, Vice Chairperson and Treasurer — were occupied by men. The secretarial position was the only one occupied by a female.

The men played a dominant role in the early years because some of them had had more exposure to disability issues from an international perspective. Wilbert Williams and Huntley Forrester, two of the first board members, studied in England and the latter had just returned home, with fresh new ideas and the desire to see disabled persons in Jamaica attain some measure of independence. In fact, he pioneered the movement here.

The men in the hierarchy of the organization represented CDA locally and internationally, and were the main spokespersons until 1987. However, women are now major players in the decision-making process of CDA — today, only two of the nine board members are male.

The men have now formed their own group, in recognition of the fact that men with disabilities have a role to play in terms of supporting the infrastructure of CDA and to counter the negative perception by society that disabled men are not being as progressive as they ought to be. Also, in light of the dominant role being played within CDA by women, they see that the men need to be more assertive, to find a new sense of direction and to change the status quo instead of being satisfied with their lot. The objective of the men's group is to be a focal point through which disabled men can address issues such as low self-esteem, personal and career development so as to become more financially self-sufficient.

Some women in leadership positions within CDA are reluctant to become involved with the CDA Women's Group. They have strong feelings that they should concern themselves with issues pertaining to persons with disabilities rather than women's issues, and they feel that there is an equal balance of power-sharing within the organization. Issues such as high unemployment, accessibility and low educational skills are shared by both men and women.

Nonetheless, the Combined Disabilities Association Women's Group has become a very integral part of the lives of many women with disabilities. The activities of the group are not limited to women from the Kingston and St. Andrew Metropolitan Area. Meetings are attended by women from Clarendon, Portland, St. Catherine and St. Thomas. We have provided a channel for women to speak out on sensitive issues, in an environment in which they feel comfortable. Through the various seminars and meetings, these women have gained a sense of self-esteem and confidence in their worth as human beings and are more willing to undertake additional responsibilities on various committees. Yet, problems remain. There is still a lack of knowledge about disabled women being subjected to domestic violence, sexual abuse and other forms of discrimination. Victims of abuse are among us, but most disabled women who are affected are not active members of the group and the few who might be are not willing to speak publicly.

For example, abusive situations have arisen in Cheshire Village. (Cheshire Village is an independent living situation where houses are built to accommodate both disabled and able-bodied persons in an integrated setting. The village is administered by the Mona Rehabilitation Centre and the houses are rented at a nominal cost to disabled and able-bodied persons. There are approximately 21 houses in the village and each accommodation can be shared by different families.) In one instance, two disabled women were beaten by their spouses. One left home and stayed with friends and returned some weeks later. The employer of the other offered her some assistance. In another recent example, a hearing-impaired girl was raped. She reported the incident to the police, who treated the matter lightly because she did not use an interpreter to relate the incident. The following day, the girl went to the training institution she attended and was quite agitated. She related the incident to a staff member, who accompanied her to the police station. The man was subsequently sent to jail. In all cases, though, these women would not speak out publicly about their experiences so not many disabled people are aware of these incidents.

Addressing the economic situation of the women is also a priority of the CDA Women's Group because the majority of us are from poor economic circumstances. Since the majority of the women in the group are unemployed, uneducated and lacking vocational skills, our priority is to obtain some means for economic independence. We think this can be achieved through membership in the group and by identifying an income-generating project which would help to strengthen us. If there is no possibility of this need being met, the group will eventually disintegrate.

Of course, we also play a very important role in providing an avenue for women with disabilities to socialize and interact with each other. In light of the importance of this, our meetings are sometimes held at places such as the Rockfort Mineral Bath, Hellshire Beach so that there is an element of recreation to our work.

Through networking and our involvement with other women's groups, women with disabilities are now being included on a national basis in activities affecting women in Jamaican society. Worthy of note was the wide cross-section of disabled women who participated in the Third All Island Conference of Women in Kingston, Jamaica, in 1992. Approximately 23 disabled women attended, with representatives from the blind, the hearing impaired and the physically disabled. Several resolutions included in the final conference document were put forward by these women. Some of the resolutions are as follows:

1. That the government institute a policy whereby all schools have special units for children with mental disabilities (mentally retarded) and children who are exceptionally gifted (genius).
2. That all tertiary institutions should be made fully accessible to the physically disabled and the visually impaired, including access to study materials (for example, braille materials, audio-taped material and readers where necessary).
3. That sign language interpretation be provided for hearing-impaired persons who meet matriculation requirements at tertiary institutions.
4. That the two percent employment quota of the government for persons with disabilities be increased to five percent and strictly adhered to.
5. That private sector companies be encouraged to apprentice women with disabilities (for example, printers, photo studios and mechanical garages).

The CDA Women's Group was also involved in the various preparatory seminars and workshops for the Fourth World Conference on Women in Beijing, China in 1995. A list of issues relating to disabled women from Jamaica was included in the final conference document.

The CDA Women's Group has worked to improve the lives of individual women with disabilities and has fought for more rights for disabled persons in Jamaica and internationally. We are proud that, because of our hard work, we have gained the respect of the Jamaican people and begun to find our place in our society.

Keny Avilés, *El Salvador*

I Have Been Born Again

I used to live locked up between four walls.
I did not know what it was like to enjoy life.
Then, one day, I had the opportunity of meeting
many people who shared my condition,
or worse.

They were always strong, they always looked ahead,
and never felt defeated.
On the contrary, they wanted to conquer,
show their true worth.

They gave my spirit strength
and taught me that life must be lived
as it manifests itself.
Taught me that we must accept ourselves
no matter what we are like, no matter our suffering.
All that counts is that we feel good about ourselves.
The rest doesn't matter.

He Vuelto a Nacer

Vivía encerrada entre cuatro paredes,
no sabía lo que era disfrutar la vida,
pero, un día tuve la oportunidad de conocer
a muchas personas que estaban en igual condición que yo,
o quizás peor.

pero seguían firmes, siempre adelante
sin sentirse vencidas,
por el contrario, querían vencer
y demostrar lo mucho que valen

y me dieron fortaleza en mi espíritu
y me enseñaron que la vida debemos de vivirla
tal y como se nos presenta,
y también que debemos aceptarnos
no importa como seamos o lo que padezcamos.
Lo importante es sentirse bien con uno mismo,
lo demás no importa.

Snapshot from Beijing
Interview by E. Catherine Boldt

Karla Krissel Rivas Rivas
*Central Association of the Blind in Guatemala,
and WK Kellogg Foundation*

As a woman, I am sure that I should have the same rights as everybody, since I am a human being. And everybody is a human being — it doesn't matter if we're men or if we're women. I think we should have the same opportunities, the same rights, and share with the men everything we have to share. I think that men are not superior to women and neither are women superior to men. We both are human beings, and, if we can work together, I think things will be better.

I want to tell all the disabled women that we should work together. That way, we can reach more goals than alone. I want to tell everybody that we are able to do many things if we really want to. It does not matter what society thinks about us. We have to show what we are able to do. I am sure that if we do it, we will reach more than we can imagine.

Irene Feika

Women with Disabilities: The Final Frontier!

It all began for me in July of 1987, with a request to attend a leadership training seminar in Jamaica. It was to be a time of shared exchanges of knowledge. I would give workshops on "Disabled Women in Leadership Roles" and "Sexuality and Disability."

In 1986, the Council of Canadians with Disabilities (CCD, formerly COPOH) had elected me as the first woman Chairperson. The significance of this was enhanced by the fact that the Disabled Peoples' International (DPI) World Council was also meeting in Ottawa. The few female DPI representatives raised this election "victory" at every opportunity and made it very clear that women were going to play an active role in the disability movement. They also emphasized the need for women with disabilities to be taught how to be leaders. It was a responsibility as well as an honour to be in this position, and that responsibility would be a guiding force in my life for years to come.

My interest in the area of sexuality and disability had evolved over the years. I knew that all people were sexual beings, but my knowledge of the issue was limited. A disabled friend and his wife had, on occasion, talked to me about putting a group together with the intent of enabling the members to become more educated in the area of human sexuality. She was a full-time teacher at the University of Alberta and he taught a course with her on sexuality during each spring session. I had taken this course and, in 1983, a group of us decided to meet on a monthly basis in order to become more knowledgeable. This eventually led to us putting on workshops and seminars. Sexuality is an area that encompasses all humanity, and I continue to take courses on it whenever they are available.

Now, fear and elation filled me in equal parts. Was I properly prepared? Would my skills be enough to assist other women with disabilities to make positive changes and take greater control over their own lives? Insecurities about my own abilities were almost overwhelming; fortunately, colleagues and friends at CCD reassured me and encouraged me to at least give it a try.

This was to be my first trip to the Caribbean, but would prove not to be my last. Jamaica: even the name triggers memories and dreams — dreams of an exotic paradise where the beauty of the land and people reigns, and memories of friendships made and ideas shared. I arrived a couple of days early and was shown the various areas that make up the city of Kingston. This was a very educational experience — seeing the poverty of tin huts and the excessive wonders of the homes of the rich. As is so often the case, I soon discovered that, just like in Canada, people with disabilities were often the poorest of the poor (and even more so if they were women with disabilities).

My learning had just begun and the training seminar would continue to teach me the realities of being disabled in developing countries. In Canada, we take many things for granted, such as access to good medical care, technical aids, medication etc. This is not always the reality in developing nations. What we do have in common with disabled people in developing countries is that the cost of these items may still prevent us from obtaining them. At one of the workshops on advocacy, we formed small groups to discuss how one can work with systems, organizations etc. I naively spoke about lobbying politicians to change the laws to include disability issues. My colleagues laughed gently and told me that, in many of their countries, as governments changed they either ignored or quickly changed laws that were perceived to be costly or in the way. For many of the people at the seminar, daily existence was a struggle. Poverty was frequently the norm and it was only through the support of family and friends that many persons with disabilities were even alive.

People from all over the Caribbean and North America spent the two weeks of the seminar hoping to educate each other about the issues, concerns and potential solutions of people with disabilities in their various homelands. New experiences and meeting new people has been, and continues to be, exciting for me. I firmly believe we can and do learn from each other. This seminar was a new experience. My first discovery was that not everyone considered adhering to rigid timelines a necessity. Workshops seldom started on time; however, once we began the learning was endless. It is interesting to note that, on the day left to the women, timelines were more closely adhered to.

My first presentation went better than I had expected. Women told me later that they could really connect with the examples I had given. I discussed the fact that, as homemakers, women already practised skills which could, with some training and hands-on experience, lead to jobs or volunteer work. Women, especially when they are also parents, manage budgets (accounting), develop schedules for the family (organization), sew and maintain clothing (craft and laundry), settle arguments (negotiation), do the shopping, often on limited budgets (market analysis and purchase) — the list of skills is endless. After this session, numerous women approached me — some to expand on the ideas and others just to talk about how their experiences as women with disabilities had affected their own lives.

My second presentation, which was on sexuality, was for both women and men and included a two-part video. The video, when properly used with other material, is a vital tool with which to open discussions about people with disabilities and sexuality. I was terrified about making this presentation because rumours had reached me that some cultures might find the topic of sexuality offensive. A couple of days before the session, I had sought out local leaders for their advice and was encouraged to hold the workshop.

The topic of sexuality and disability is one that opens unexplored areas. It is as if, by "giving permission" to talk about what is frequently considered to be a forbidden zone, we give ourselves permission to discuss all aspects of our lives. Although I had done numerous sessions on sexuality prior to this, and have done many since, the one in Jamaica stands out in my mind as a very special time of shared learning. A number of women who attended have told me this workshop changed how they felt about themselves. They have talked about the fact that they finally realized sexuality is a very basic part of being human (disabled or not). Some said the session raised their self-esteem while others stated it felt so good to be able to discuss openly what is all too often a taboo subject for people with disabilities. For me, it was an experience that showed how close we as human beings really can be, in spite of the differences of our cultures. Due to many requests, I am now always prepared to do a session on sexuality and disability whenever I leave Canada.

The following year, the Dominica Association held a series of workshops specifically to address women's issues. This also proved to be a vibrant and vital time of sharing and learning for me. At the disabled women's conference in Dominica, approximately one-third of the participants were male; the women had decided this would be an opportunity to teach men with disabilities about some of the needs specific to women with disabilities. I had been requested to do a full-day workshop on sexuality. After some discussion, it was decided that Francine Arsenault (another Canadian) and I would do a combined workshop on The Role of the Family and Sexuality and Disability. This workshop led to numerous discussions. Many of the women from the Caribbean nations also led workshops such as the Role of the Woman in the Family, Education and Disability, Family Planning etc. The topics were not always gender specific and caused many a challenging discussion.

After Dominica, I was asked to return to Jamaica to meet with a variety of women with disabilities. The women members of the Jamaican Combined Disabilities Association had requested through CCD that I meet with them to further discuss the role of women in the Disabled Consumer Movement. Throughout the world, people with disabilities have been organizing our own groups, where we act as the decision makers. In the past, all decisions were made by organizations that provided us with services and were ruled by others — hence the term "consumer." The purpose, as we understood it, for these meetings was to empower Jamaican women with disabilities to become more involved in their disability organizations at a decision-making level.

Upon arriving in Kingston, I phoned the Combined Disabilities Association office and, by chance, got the current Chairperson, who set up a series of meetings with other women with disabilities. I suggested using my hotel room as a meeting place or going to the most convenient location for the women. In the end, we did both.

The first group of three women came to the hotel; they had chosen a spokesperson from among themselves in order to address specific issues and concerns. She was direct and to the point, stating that, at first, they had not wanted to come but, on hearing that I, too, was disabled, they decided to give it a try. She explained that a variety of people had come to them in the past to do research and had always promised to send copies of the reports and keep in touch, but never did so. They all hoped another women with a disability would be more reliable. Then came the big question: "What exactly was my disability?" This is not an uncommon question, as my disabilities are of the hidden variety. I told them, "Diabetes, arthritis, asthma and a gastrointestinal system that does not work."

Once these preliminaries were out of the way, we were able to communicate. The women had decided they would each speak with me individually and the balcony proved to be a great place for this. After private discussions, we got together and talked about some common concerns and ideas. It was great. We talked and listened to each other and, as is wont to happen, recognized that our humanity was really what counted. The best thing that came out of this meeting was the friendships we have to this day. These women have, over the years, added great joy to my life and continue to help me in my understanding of the perils and pressures women with disabilities must overcome.

Not all meetings took place in the hotel; I was invited to meet with disabled women in the community, too. One of these meetings was with a group of blind women who held a dance class after work. I was able to observe the last few minutes of their dancing, which was both graceful and, for them, a lot of fun. What I remember most was a gesture of kindness and respect made by one of the women just prior to beginning our meeting. The dancers had changed back into their street clothes and were gaily talking patois to each other about their day. One woman quietly admonished the others, stating clearly that I probably did not understand patois and they should speak what I could understand. It was a small, but, to me, a very meaningful comment.

The actual meeting was very informal and our curiosity about each other kept conversations going. We talked about the things women have discussed for millenia when there are no men present: partners, children, the difficulties of single parenting, employment and what it is like to be a woman with a disability in our societies today. They shared both joy and grief, relating how, all too frequently, the men they met through work or school wanted them as sexual partners, but would seldom want to marry them. Some of the women had children and discussed the problems as well as the joys of being a single parent. It was a topic I could easily relate to, having been a single parent myself. These women, in spite of their disability, were very independent. They shared their hopes and their dreams — their hopes for good jobs and a nice home and their dreams of meeting a good, kind person to marry and share their lives with.

I also met disabled women who worked in the community. Some were well educated and held professional positions, others were in jobs where they received training, while still others were working at upgrading or getting a better education. All had a common goal: They wanted to be accepted by society as people first, whose disability was merely another aspect of their humanity. This was an interesting time for me, as women with disabilities in Canada go through the same processes. One thing I did learn was that the disabled women in Jamaica had to be more creative in order to survive, as they did not have the social programmes we in Canada accept as our right.

Family and friends are vital to the existence of Jamaican women with disabilities, for they may be the only road to survival. Governments all too frequently do not make provisions for people with disabilities and therefore their very existence may depend on the financial as well as physical support of their friends and/or families. This is reality. Consequently, education is very important, particularly when one considers that jobs for people with disabilities are difficult to come by at the best of times. Children with disabilities are all too often excluded from an adequate education. For example, one disabled woman with whom I correspond on a regular basis told me she is not sure how she learned to read and write as she has never attended school.

During this particular trip, I also met a deaf woman who wanted information on legislation in Canada about driving. She had heard that deaf people were able to obtain drivers' licences in Canada. Through CCD I was able to send her the requested information and it is my understanding she did eventually obtain her own licence. In dealing with women who are deaf I also met sign language interpreters; one of them was a woman who eventually came to my home in Sherwood Park while attending university in the city of Edmonton (which is about a twenty-minute drive from where I live). This young woman was working on her degree in sign interpretation, not only to be able to interpret, but also to be able to teach other interpreters in the Caribbean. She spoke of the great need for real communication systems for people who are deaf and reinforced the fact that sign language is just that — a language.

Some of the women I met at the Mona Rehabilitation Center in Jamaica told me their experiences living there were very positive. One young disabled woman put it in perspective for me. She stated that living there had given her the first experiences with other people with disabilities, and the realization that she was not the only disabled child in Jamaica really helped her to cope, not only with her limitations but also with the teasing and negative comments she had had to put up with before. As a Canadian disabled person, I had thought only of the negative side of institutional living; the disabled women of Jamaica made me aware that even institutions can, for some disabled people, be a positive influence.

One of the many things I learned from disabled Jamaican women is that it is important to put things in perspective. I also learned that what works in one society may not work in another. This is not to say we should not share concepts or programmes, but we should encourage and accept that numerous adaptations may be needed in order for them to work in another culture.

During a couple of my consultations in Jamaica, I was able to visit Diversified Economic Enterprise for Disabled Self-help (DEEDS) Industries. This is a factory operation that makes a variety of wooden artifacts and employs many people with disabilities in a profitable venture. I found it of great interest that some of the disabled women are working in traditionally male occupations such as that of lathe operator. The various artifacts they make are of the finest quality.

On my various trips back to Jamaica it has become very clear to me that disabled women are consistently taking on stronger roles and becoming leaders within the disabled consumer movement. They are chairing organizations, committees and meetings, while continuing to work and raise families. They also hold regular "rap" sessions where people with disabilities can share their ideas and concerns.

My Jamaican friends and I have shared a great deal over the years of my involvement and I continue to learn from them, as I hope they do from me. Through my consultations and involvement I have also met women with disabilities from other Caribbean nations with whom I have shared thoughts and ideas. There is so much we can learn from one another. No one person, culture or country has all the answers when it comes to disability issues. However, as women with disabilities, we are all first and foremost human beings who can and do learn from one another. It is my hope that, in the years to come, we disabled women will continue to strive for a better life for all people with disabilities.

Joyce Joseph, *Trinidad and Tobago*

Who Am I

What do you see when you look at me?
Can you see the beauty that lies within me?
I am hidden within a twisted frame,
Wanting so much to proclaim,
> *Who I am.*

What do you see when we meet?
That my shape is not all that neat.
The posture just is not complete,
As I can't stand on my two feet.
> *Who am I?*

What do you hear when I speak?
Words of comfort or of pain.
Words you'll want to hear again,
Or maybe you can't stand the strain.
> *Who am I?*

What do you feel when we touch?
Emotions that don't feel like much.
Surprise to find that I am of Him divine,
And someday you will find and know...
> *Who I am.*

Ruth Rodríguez, *El Salvador*

Melancholy

I felt your strong warm hands
barely touch mine.
Not a word was uttered
just glances,
a stare that penetrates
and makes me imagine
those idyllic moments
we could spend together
feeling your body next to mine.
I imagined that
you would feel this same trembling
But no:

In the end it is always the same,
see you soon and no more.

Melancolia

Sentir tus manos fuertes y tibias
rozando suavemente las mias
sin decir palabra alguna
y tan solo las miradas ...
esas miradas ... tan penetrantes
que me hacen pensar
idíilicos momentos
que podríamos pasar, y
sentir tu cuerpo junto a mi cuerpo
llegue a creer que
sentirías el estremecimiento
que en mí surgía,
pero no...

Al final siempre es lo mismo
un hasta pronto y ... nada más.

K-Lynn, *Canada*

Passion Fruit

Bruised assumed bitter
left
unsqueezed unsampled
cast aside
without being tasted
although
ripe, sweet, juicy
squirts of amber appetite
its core
delectable

Eileen Girón Batres

To Speak is Empowering: Literacy Project for Women with Disabilities in El Salvador

Once upon a time ...

> *There was a young girl with a disability. When she was a teenager, she never talked about boyfriends or the boys she liked. She talked a lot with her girl-friends about the boys they liked. But everyone assumed that she did not have anything to say about relationships between herself and the boys. Years later she realized that her friends saw her as an asexual being because of her disability. Even about the issue of disability, it seemed there was nothing to talk about. Keeping so many things to herself for a long time, without having anyone to share them with, was very painful.*

This was one of my reasons for wanting to start a women's programme: I always wondered how many women with disabilities were going through the same painful experiences as I was. Why not get together and share our thoughts among ourselves? I wanted to bring women with disabilities together, to encourage them to talk about themselves, about their fears, their needs.

A WOMEN'S PROGRAMME WITHIN AN ORGANIZATION OF MEN AND WOMEN

The Asociación Cooperativa del Grupo Independiente Pro Rehabilitacion Integral (ACOGIPRI) began in El Salvador in 1981 as a cooperative association. Seven of us conceived of the idea of starting a ceramics cooperative as an income-generating project for persons with disabilities. It all began because we knew a severely disabled woman who only had the use of one hand and could not find work. I was the only one of the seven who did not have a job, so I became the first chairperson of ACOGIPRI, coordinating our many different activities. I have been very closely involved with the cooperative and the ceramics workshop since it started.

In the beginning, there were around 18 young men and women in the ceramics workshop. Their disabilities were different — some were paraplegics, some had polio, others were deaf and a couple were partially blind. They all received the same opportunities for the training, but for reasons such as over-protection from their parents, taking care of the household or just having too many problems in their romantic experiences, the young women were not as constant in their attendance as the young men. Six years later, the ceramics workshop had turned into a small business. The young men and women had become workers and had developed very good skills, but only three women remained in the workshop. One woman who was deaf was an excellent worker, but suddenly decided she was going away.

At the same time, I was looking at women's roles within our organization. ACOGIPRI had been an affiliate member of Disabled Peoples' International (DPI). As part of the Latin American region, we participated in the regional meetings. As far back as I could remember, our voices as women had never been listened to. I remembered having listened to very long and good speeches, from my colleagues — all of them men. I always thought, "I wish I could speak like that," but I was afraid to speak up because I thought I did not have much to say. I also was afraid that my vocabulary was just not good enough. I was behaving as a "perfect woman."

It became very clear to me that something was happening to women with disabilities in terms of being employed. But it was not only the issue of employment — the problem went beyond that. It involved issues of relationships, about having a family, about participating in the community activities, about empowering, about making decisions. My wish to develop a programme for women was reinforced.

THE LITERACY PROJECT

From 1987 onwards, women from ACOGIPRI searched for other women with disabilities to come to our meetings. At first, we were only three women. One worked in the administration at the cooperative, the other was a psychologist friend of mine, and I was the only one who had a disability. We would discuss what issue we wanted to talk about. We learned about the book *Imprinting our Image* — which is a collection of articles written by women with disabilities from different parts of the world — from Diane Driedger, one of the editors of the book. After some discussions with Diane, the idea of a literacy project for women with disabilities in the Central American region was born, which led in 1987 to the creation of the Literacy Project for Women with Disabilities.

Once I had found out that we would get funding for the project, I asked Ruth Rodriguez, who was just starting to participate in our group, if she wanted to be the Literacy Project coordinator. Ruth accepted, which was very good for her and for the programme. At our many different meetings, we always had someone who participated very actively in the programme.

The Literary Project was very ambitious and very important. Central American countries have no cultural tradition of reading. In 1972 there was educational reform, but, after more than twenty years, it was discovered that this reform had made the educational system worse. Among other things, the average person who had finished primary school during this period was not able to write reports, articles or other material. A literacy project for women with disabilities was difficult to imagine. Still, we asked ourselves: Was there any other way to talk about women with disabilities if we were not going to do it for ourselves? We decided that there was no other way.

In the planning for the project, many issues other than literacy had to be considered — issues such as self-esteem and gender. As well, the search for more women with disabilities willing to join us continued. There were many eligible women, but not all of them wanted to participate. Some were not prepared to go out of their homes, where they were very well taken care of and where they were just fine watching TV, not making decisions. But, eventually, the search for women was successful. They were found in the capital city of San Salvador and in other Salvadoran cities and in other countries such as Guatemala, Nicaragua, Costa Rica, Panama and Mexico.

As the training started, women began to write — although not all the women wrote and there weren't many articles or poems. The writing that did occur was brought together in a newsletter and the newsletter was sent to all the women who had been interested in the project. Not every woman was ready to write an article, but some were ready to speak about things they had kept to themselves for so many years. Simply to be able to speak was empowering.

WOMEN HAVING THEIR SAY

Participation in this project not only brought women with disabilities together, it also led to us getting together with other groups of women. There was so much energy put into the project — it was like switching on thousands of light bulbs. One of the participants, Maritza Melara, said, "It was like some light in the darkness, one light after the other and so on. Suddenly we were so many women together, laughing, thinking, sharing, but most of all fighting — fighting against everything that had been *denied* to us, opening the doors of knowledge to recover our condition as human beings. Having participated in the Literacy Project for Women with Disabilities has been one of the highlights of my life, because it has helped me to understand that being a person, or a woman, with a disability does not mean accepting anything without questioning; instead, we have to try to transform or change our segregated reality into opportunities for individuals and for groups. I have learned a lot, especially because I have shared with other women, but also because it has been very gratifying to work with my fellow women."

Another interesting experience came from Cecilia Contreras, who is physically disabled. She attended a special education school, but never finished her primary school. Considering that the average Salvadoran does not read and therefore very seldom writes, Cecilia's case is really special. She participated in some of the training courses of the Literacy Project. Two years later, she started to write a short story — a love story about a woman with a disability.

Ruth Rodriguez, the project coordinator, explained what the project has meant: "When I was asked to work on the project, I thought I was not able to do it, because my self- esteem was so low after my cerebral disease. But I accepted. I started out with lots of fear. Usually when I had to go out, I had someone from my family with me. At work I had to be by myself. I had to face so many barriers — they were architectural as well as attitudinal barriers that I met with for the first time, because at home I was very well protected. I started to realize that the world outside was different and I had to deal with it in order to improve my work and my personal life. I learned a lot. Working with other women and participating in so many activities helped me to recover my self-esteem. Through the project, I had the opportunity to meet more friends, to visit other countries, to meet other organizations of persons with disabilities, to be involved in the women's movement. I was able to help a lot of women. This was very rewarding."

Angelica Monteagudo talked about her experience in the following way: "My participation in the Literacy Project was writing and editing the newsletters. This has been a learning experience. Reading the poems and the stories of women with disabilities has made me aware of the way they face their problems and needs, how they see life. There is no need to be very intellectual to express what we feel and want. The workshops have been very successful. They have helped us a lot, as a means of popular expression and also as a place where women's voices are listened to. What has been more productive is that our articles have reached many women in the whole country, as well as in neighbouring countries. We are certain that women have felt reassured, as we have read in their correspondence to us. What is also pleasant is that there is always a space for my articles and poems. Maybe this sounds simple, but for me it is very important. I am sure that the women who read my articles will be encouraged to write, too. Plus, we have a place to talk about our rights, our failures, our successes and joys."

IMPACT OF THE PROJECT WITHIN
THE ORGANIZATION

Putting so much energy into a woman's project within ACOGIPRI, an organization with three men and two women on its Board of Directors, did create some tension at the beginning. There were questions, such as, "Why spend so much money on women only?" This question was also asked by a funder. The question was fair, but our answer to that question was: "Women with disabilities are not included in any programme at all — they deserve more projects like this one." Within ACOGIPRI, this statement was very well understood. Our male colleagues were absorbing the concepts of gender, self-esteem and so on at the same time as we were. We recognize that they played a very important role in the development of the project, to the point where, without their support and understanding, the project would not have been as successful as it was. It is important to note, though, that the decisions about the project were always taken by women.

ACOGIPRI is the only organization of men and women with disabilities in El Salvador that has a women's programme. Because of this, some other organizations have not wanted to work on joint programmes. But they are only a minority, because many groups are beginning to understand how important it is to work for women's development.

In the history of the organizations of persons with disabilities in Central America, the Literacy Project will be remembered as the starting point — the opportunity for women with disabilities to realize that our needs are different. From now on, those who develop programmes for persons with disabilities will have to consider our specific needs in the planning process. Women are now aware that we have to speak up to be heard.

IMPACT OF THE PROJECT IN THE COMMUNITY

Being an activist for the rights of persons with disabilities can be very rewarding, but at the same time it can be very frustrating. A person involved with this issue for a long time tends to forget that the general population lives in a world where there are no disabled people. Once we get out of our homes and our organizations, we find out that our communities are not prepared for us. There have been cases where ramps were built for us, but a single step had to be climbed to access that ramp, or cars were parked right in front of the ramp.

Looking for an accessible place to hold the training for the Literacy Project was also work. Some hotels looked very accessible, but the toilets were totally inaccessible. In one instance, a woman in a wheelchair fell down trying to go to the toilet in a five star hotel. This is one of the reasons why a severely disabled woman does not want to go out of her house — it makes sense. But on the other hand, how can we change things if we remain invisible? The answer is simple: by being there.

As part of the project, we went from one place to another for training and to participate in different activities. This was during the end of the war in El Salvador — a time when there was a boom in non-disabled women's organizations and a general awareness of the need to fight for women's rights. As a result, in 1993 a large number of women formed a group called MUJERES '94 (WOMEN '94). They worked on a document to present to all political parties as part of their Plan of Action for the presidential elections in 1994. We attended every single invitation we received from this and other groups of women. For the first time in the history of El Salvador, women with disabilities were included in the most important document about women ever written by the women of El Salvador. This happened because one of our members was always present in the discussions. It is not an exaggeration to affirm that, without the Literacy Project, we would not even have noticed that this political movement was happening in our city.

Many other events followed, and they were also included in the project. In 1993, we participated in two big international congresses — the Fifth Multidisciplinary Women's Congress in Costa Rica and the Sixth Latin American and Caribbean Feminist Meeting in

El Salvador. These are just some of the outstanding activities of the women's programme in the last two years. Looking back to the time when we were planning for the Literacy Project, we can see that the way it turned out has gone beyond our expectations. It not only provided training, it raised the awareness, among disabled and non-disabled women alike, about gender issues and the way they affect us — women with disabilities.

THE FOURTH WORLD CONFERENCE ON WOMEN IN BEIJING

Early in 1994, the women's group of ACOPIPRI participated in a big meeting called by the United Nations Developing Programme to elect the National Committee of non-governmental organizations who were to represent our country at the Fourth World Conference on Women. I was surprised to be one of the women elected. As a representative of ACOGIPRI, I was involved in the preparatory activities for the conference. A document on disabled women and violence, called for by the First Lady of El Salvador, was prepared for the National Forum which preceded the Beijing conference. At the forum, a woman in the audience said that she was surprised to see a woman in a wheelchair representing women with disabilities — she had thought we would not have anything to say about the conference; instead, she found she learned a lot from our presentation. The final document was taken to Beijing by our official delegation.

EPILOGUE

It is difficult to describe how much was accomplished in a three-year period with a few words. The book we hoped to publish was never written — although this might happen later — but some of the poetry in this book was written as part of our project. From my perspective, the great success of the project was in empowering the women with disabilities who participated in the project. This would have never been possible without the support of Diane Driedger, the CCD, other funders and friends. On behalf of our women's programme, I express our gratitude to all of them.

Eileen Girón Batres, *El Salvador*

Poem To A Body

Small, twisted and deformed: such is my body.
Incapable of inspiring a love poem.
Incapable of setting fire to a night of passion.
A man once said to me:
       "Your eyes are beautiful."
He did not want to add:
       "In spite of your body."

Do you want to know something?
that body,
small, twisted and deformed:
It is mine and I love it,
I have no other!

Poema De Un Cuerpo

Pequeño, torcido y deforme es mi cuerpo.
Incapaz de inspirar un poema de amor.
Incapaz de encender una noche de pasion.
Un hombre me dijo una vez:
       "Tienes ojos bonitos"
No quiso agregar:
       "A pesar de tu cuerpo"

Saben que?
Ese cuerpo, pequeño, torcido y deforme
me encanta y lo quiero. Es el mio.
No tengo otro!

Eudalie Wickham

Rhythms and Heartbeats: A Poetry Workshop

As a teenager I was painfully shy and found it extremely difficult to express myself verbally to other persons. Then I fell in love with the literary arts; I'd found one of my heartbeats. I started to write poems and short stories to release the pulsating rhythms within me. I use my imagination and emotions to express in poetry my visions of adventure and happenings around and within me.

For this reason, I was extremely excited about attending the four-day poetry workshop organized by the Disabled Women's Network of Trinidad and Tobago (DAWN T&T). This workshop was successful! Both the participants and the organization were strengthened by this experience. Many of us learned of the importance of sustaining our work and that of our organizations. Several of the participants commented on the fact that they were able to work as part of a team and manage the coordination of the workshop. With these newly learned skills and its stronger self-confidence, DAWN T&T will be able to build a more viable organization.

The atmosphere at the Emmaus Centre, where the workshop was held, was conducive to self-expression

60

and creative writing. The serenity of the centre allowed us to feel at peace with ourselves, and attuned to our Divine Maker. Those four days were spent in a garden of lush, green grass, a mirage of colourful flowers and musical creatures. This was renewal time — a time for us to analyse our roles as leaders, role models, mothers and sisters, and to recommit ourselves to moving forward confidently.

Some people hold the view that workshops and seminars of this nature are just talkshops, but participants at this poetry workshop share a different, less skeptical opinion. Many of us saw the power that lies within us and the inner strength that has made us the individuals that we are. Ever so often, we need to remind ourselves — or be reminded — that life is full of opportunities and blessings, and that we are free to make adjustments to change and improve our lives.

In every disabled person's life there is some measure of frustration and struggle. In the workshop, many of the struggles and frustrations were discussed with the use of poetry. Written and spoken words told of being abused by a family member and having other family members pretend that it never happened. The poetic words told of being betrayed, and feeling so ashamed and afraid that nothing was said or done for years, until the struggle to keep it within was lost. Even then, brothers, sisters and others refused to help. Again, dramatic words told of the struggle to live an independent life, and of seeking to manage personal affairs, but being smothered or victimized because of this desire. All of this makes it crucial for persons with disabilities to be frank in our discussions about our fight for self-preservation.

Sharing the possibility of what can be achieved through self-mastery, and growing together through fellowships such as we experienced in this workshop, is important to us women with disabilities. In nightly rap sessions, we spoke of our needs, our fears and our aspirations. The bonding of our spirits helped us to share these sacred secrets. I learnt how to open myself and share a little more of my deepest thoughts and writings.

Prior to attending the poetry workshop, I had never viewed my poetry very seriously. I thought of my creative writing merely as a way of finding self-expression on subjects I had intense feelings about. However, before the conclusion of the workshop, I was able to share my work more easily with others and I was convinced that my creative writing was definitely an area I needed to develop.

As women with disabilities attending this poetry workshop, many of us saw ourselves (sometimes for the first time) as sensual, intelligent human beings. Through this art form of self-awareness and expression, we grew closer together, drawing strength from each other while in Trinidad. One woman told us of her struggle to adjust to losing her sight and shared her feelings about being afraid and her sisters not understanding or appreciating her fears or concerns. In writing about this struggle, she was able to allay some of her fears and loneliness.

One sister of whom I feel very proud is Lustra (not her real name) who allowed the other participants' zest for life and friendship to touch her life. Her shyness, which blanketed her pain and fear, began to erode after two days of hearing non-stop conversations from her roommates. Their soliciting her opinions on their dress and so on made her realize that she was needed and appreciated. It was clear that Lustra's self-esteem was boosted through her inter-action with us at this historic meeting — she was at ease with other performers and creative writers. As a result of the staging of this special session, Lustra later wrote of her disability, experiences and renewed interest in life.

I also met a woman there whom I felt was a younger sister. We spoke deeply and honestly about our pasts and other topics; many secrets were revealed — secrets which needed to be released at that exact moment and which reflected on our lives, our choices and challenges. This was a time of healing and moving ahead. We reaffirmed our committment to living each day joyously. It was delightful to talk and write in the solitude of the Emmaus Centre; it was a balm to our creative souls.

When we are receptive, we are conscious of the happenings around us and realize that we feel passionately about certain issues. Our minds become active and we become creative — hence we write poems and perform dramatic acts. Often, submerged feelings come to the fore. In Trinidad, we understood that creative writing is a medium wherein we learn who we truly are and can educate others. Caribbean women have been using this forum to demand better living conditions, and we are now doing likewise.

I felt no barriers, no intolerance or hostility as I read my poetry or listened to others. On one occasion, we were treated to a beautiful oral poem showcasing Tobago. As we listened to the poet's rich melodious voice describing this island in the Caribbean, we saw the lush scenery, vibrant culture and heard the noises of tropical life in our mind's eyes. Every day was fresh with teachings about realizing our talents, assessing our work and structuring our prose. Wonderful results were achieved through this workshop — feelings of rejection and inferiority experienced by women with disabilities were transformed into assurance and assertiveness. Some of the local women learned new skills, such as how to coordinate such an event, how to work as part of a team and how to be dependable. Our able-bodied instructors learned more about women with disabilities, realizing quickly that we were not as "different" as we are often portrayed to be.

Some people believe that only certain persons have talents while others are not so lucky. However, it was clear to all the participants in the workshop that we all have talents. Altogether this workshop was poetry at its best — it allowed the bonding of spirits, mutual encouragement, the sharing of words and love, and the emergence of stronger women.

Eudalie Wickham, *Barbados*

A Poet's Thought

To persevere
helps us to reach the mountain top,
or cross the grand old sea.
Yes, perseverance is good,
for it helps us to behold thoughts
that would break the barriers,
barriers of intolerance and discrimination.
Oh, perseverance makes the advocacy dream live;
a dream once awakened will not be
dampened or put out.

To persevere
helps us to be faithful to the cause
and battle each new heartache and pain,
changing them into jewels of triumph.
Yes, perseverance
helps us to walk around an island
or stand just three with our placards,
or look in the mirror and reflect,
determined to leave a bright mark in this wonderful world!

Maritza Melara Castillo, *El Salvador*

Confession

I cannot run
Yet each road has its goal.
I cannot dance to rock and roll, or jazz, or pop
And yet
I enjoy the music intensely.
I cannot walk alone to the edges of the sea
Yet the surging movement of the waves inspires me
The sunsets thrill me
The immensity of sky and water shakes me.
To sit on the sand, to see the gulls, to greet the sun,
To listen to the complaints of silence ... and to laugh ... and to weep ...
Gives me the assurance that I am alive ... gives me life ...
To smile at a passer-by, take up a pencil, speak your name,
To feel you melt me with your look, discover me behind the shyness,
Bend my defences.
I hear your voice.
How tiny and how huge I am!
I make the moon mine, when I dream
And yet
Tomorrow frightens me ...
I want to steal glances
How it would pain me to lose yours.
I adore children ...
Their laughter, their games, their strangeness, wit and wisdom ...
I would like to be able to say one day: "I have caressed my child, my friend.
I have had a share of that most beautiful emotion."
Nevertheless
I know that I have loved
Have felt, have thought
Have lived it all.
All has been possible
And even more
Lover, and I think there is ... still more.

Donna M. Sinclair, *Jamaica*

I Have Potential

I have potential
I am a person of worth
There are many things I can do
With my hands, my voice,
My mind too.
I am creative, talented,
Unique.

It may be that you see
Only my disability
When you look at me, but
Accept me for who I am
Then tell me
Who do you see?

Don't you see a bright,
Aspiring, active person?
Don't you see a person
Who shows promise?

I am human, soulful and true.
The azure sky
Spreads wide and far
I reach for my star
And there seems no limit
To the successes I can achieve.

So don't call me
Cripple, handicap, worthless idiot.
I am a vibrant, aspiring, talented,
Unique person of worth
And I have potential.

Snapshot from Beijing
Interview by E. Catherine Boldt

Maomy Ruth Esiba
United Disabled Persons of Kenya

Women in Africa do not have their rights, especially in the rural areas. It is like we are second to men. Disabled women do not know about their rights. They look on themselves as very unfortunate people. When you are not educated, you do not have an opportunity to get out of your environment — so you do not know what is happening. A few of us who were a bit fortunate, who have gone to school, we have taken it upon ourselves to make sure every disabled woman knows about what is happening with women, especially with their rights.

We are still at the initial stages. We hope, with time, that we are going to reach every disabled woman in our country. That is our duty, though we have not done it yet. But we hope to do it. It is a big job. We just pray — we need the grace of God — otherwise we cannot manage it on our own.

We are professionals elsewhere, so this is voluntary work. We have started out very well: To manage to pay for someone to go to Beijing — like myself — that is quite something.

My philosophy is that my disability will never stop me from achieving what I want to achieve. Even if it means climbing on a building, I will struggle. I have always told people: I am not going to sit back and be oppressed and look miserable because I am disabled. I'm going to fight along with the others. I want to be like any other woman. If they go to school, I also go to school. If they get jobs, I also get jobs. When they are going places, I accompany them. I didn't want anyone to tell me that because I am disabled they don't want me.

Lorraine Thomas, *Trinidad and Tobago*

Life in Trinidad and Tobago

When will we
realize that
Ah, our land is
Beautiful?
     We chop up
Turtles,
and desecrate
full
spate
our beaches
Then want to
Know why
Tourists
pass
us
by.

Come Carnival
We have glorious fun
in the sun
And live on the
Run
For two days
Until it is Lent.
Then, with heads
Bent
We repent
And wait for the
Next baby boom.

We treat our women
strangely.
It is a compliment

To get a
"Psst,"
A villanous
Hiss,
Smut
or any such
Rot.
You Trinidad men.
Machoists.

We have vagrants.
A few are
flagrant.
Others do no harm,
But nonetheless,
They pee,
Spit
Harass
Beg
Sleep and
Deface the place.
We don't do
Anything
About it.

Walking down the street
Listening to the beat
of
Rap
    and
Dub
Looking at feet
Coated with
L.A. Gear
Espying a man
With pill box hair.
Geez,
Is this
Trinidad or
Washington, D.C.?

Exasperation,
Frustration,
And sometimes
Desperation.
We migrate
Because we cannot
Tolerate
This country's
Slackness
Ineptitude
or impoverished
Attitude
   Anymore.

But still,
We love
Trinidad.

Diane Driedger &
Kathleen Guy

Begrudging Acceptance: Gender Relations in the Trinidad and Tobago Chapter of Disabled Peoples' International

"Maude" is in her seventies and newly blind. She is an active member of the Disabled Women's Network of Trinidad and Tobago (DAWN T&T) and does most of her household chores herself. She finds that she has problems mostly with the male members of her family. She lives with her grown son and his wife and children. Her teenage grandson often takes her possessions and uses them. When asked, he is either reluctant to admit what he's doing or he denies what he has done. Her son has come to the conclusion that "this blind woman" is the cause of the young man's misdemeanors and accuses her of not liking him. The young man is seldom corrected for what he does.

"Mary" is a forty-two year old disabled woman. She became disabled when she was a teenager, as a result of violence. She is a hard worker. At the sheltered workshop where she works, she is one of the best workers. She lives with her husband, who is also physically disabled. Up until a few months ago, Mary was an alcoholic. She has now quit and is trying hard not to begin drinking again. Her husband is an alcoholic and treats her violently and disrespectfully most of the time. Recently, her teenage son was killed in a shooting accident. She has not recovered fully from this grief. Her daughter, who has a child but still lives at home, is also abusive and disrespectful.

"Jane" is a working, physically disabled woman. She is married and lives with her husband in a suburban area outside of the city. She is happy in her job as a school teacher. She was trained at the university and now is quite successful. She is a good example of someone who has integrated into society and is doing well. Her husband, who went to school with her, is quite attentive and is an active member of many volunteer organizations, including those for physically disabled persons. At work, he trains teachers and children to work with physically disabled students.

INTRODUCTION

Gender relations are beginning to change all over the world. The disabled community of Trinidad and Tobago has been working on this issue in the last four years. The Disabled Women's Network of Trinidad and Tobago has been particularly active. Persons with disabilities have been ignored and hidden away with few opportunities the world over, and this is very true in the Caribbean as well. Women with disabilities experience the double oppression of being disabled and being women in a society where both groups are discriminated against. We will outline the growth of disabled persons' organizations and their inclusion of disabled women's concerns by tracing the growth of the Disabled Women's Network of Trinidad and Tobago (DAWN T&T). Finally, we will discuss the impact of DAWN T&T on gender relations in the Trinidad and Tobago Chapter of Disabled Peoples' International (DPI T&T), which includes both men and women.

THE SITUATION OF DISABLED PERSONS

Disabled persons in Trinidad and Tobago are — as they are in all parts of the world — the poorest of the poor. While Trinidad is a country that has been more prosperous than other Caribbean nations because of the oil boom, disabled persons still live in poverty. There is a social assistance system, but it does not pay well and barely maintains the individual. Most disabled persons are unemployed and lack opportunities to receive training.

The difficulties in obtaining employment exist partly because of inaccessible workplaces and transportation systems. There is no accessible public transportation for disabled persons. Some disabled persons who attempt to take public taxis and buses encounter stairs that they must climb. If they use a wheelchair, they cannot use buses at all. Blind persons who ride taxis are at the mercy of the driver as to whether they will be offered a ride or not. Women with disabilities, in particular, have cited numerous instances of being verbally harassed by public transport drivers. One blind woman reported that a driver told her she should "stay at home because girls like you have no business being outside the home." This is an indicator of the overall public attitude: Disabled persons are incapable invalids and cannot participate in society like everyone else.

Many disabled persons have only an elementary school education. This situation is due to the lack of transportation, the inaccessibility of schools and the attitudes of their families. Although some parents carried their disabled children to school or pulled them along in a small cart, as soon as the children grew too big, they stopped going to school. Buses are inaccessible and a mobility impaired child cannot walk long distances. Often, families feel it is not important to educate a disabled person because he or she will not amount to anything in life anyway. If there are opportunities to go to special schools for the blind or the deaf, it is usually boys who receive them.

As for housing, it is difficult for mobility impaired persons to find places to live. One person leaves his wheelchair with the people who live in a downstairs apartment and crawls up three flights of stairs to his place. As well, the demand for wheelchairs and other mobility appliances far outstrips the numbers of those available. Not only are the few appliances costly, they are also hard to obtain.

Overall, women with disabilities are even more discriminated against than men. They are in a situation of double jeopardy — they are disabled *and* women in a society which discriminates against both. Women with disabilities often bear the brunt of physical, sexual and emotional violence within the family home. It is quite common for disabled girls to be molested by male family members, who say: "No one will want you anyway, so we might as well have you." In situations such as this, the girl is terrorized, often for her whole life, because she is shut in the home and has no one else to support her emotionally or financially. She is isolated. She begins to believe that the abuse may be all right because she will never have sex with any other man.

In other cases, disabled women experience emotional abuse in the family through taunts such as "You are worthless and living off us." Family members sometimes take away anything the woman does own. Several blind women report that their things are often moved or taken by family members — and often the family denies that they have taken the things for themselves.

Other women with disabilities who are married and became disabled during the marriage report physical violence from their spouses. In addition, some husbands force their wives to stay at home as shut-ins.

There are few choices for disabled women in abusive situations. They often do not have the financial or emotional support to leave. And, in any case, where would they go? There is only one women's shelter in the country, and it is inaccessible.

DISABLED PEOPLE ORGANIZE

The disabled peoples' movement in Trinidad and Tobago is beginning to initiate change for disabled persons, both men and women. It started out by forming a leisure and sports club and moved on to build an organization for self-representation and advocacy.

The first organization composed of people with disabilities — the Pioneers Sports and Leisure Club — was founded in North Trinidad in 1977. This group has attracted many disabled youth, both women and men, through the years. Social gatherings are held once a month and sports activities have also been organized. Some disabled persons in the club are employed and serve as role models

for the others. The group has benefited the participants by providing feelings of belonging, self-esteem and inspiration — feelings
that come from meeting other people with disabilities who are
"making it" in the world. The club has also offered opportunities
for participation in the International Games for the Disabled. In
1984, it fielded its first team to the games in New York. Several
members of the club, both men and women, won medals at the
games.

The Pioneers has served as a training ground for future leaders
in the advocacy movement. They obtained skills in fundraising by
sending their delegates to overseas sports events and they learned
skills in management and organization by working within their
group. Some of the young people from the Pioneers moved on to
help found the Trinidad and Tobago Chapter of Disabled Peoples'
International (DPI T&T) in 1986. Since then, DPI T&T has played
a role in discussing legislation for the inclusion of disabled persons
in society and DPI T&T representatives have attended government
meetings concerning a comprehensive legislation on the rights of
disabled persons.

Central to the organization of both groups has been Kenwyn
Rodriguez, a wheelchair user and leader in the disability community for over 15 years. Looking back over the last ten years, Rodriguez notes that the major achievement of the movement is that
there is now more awareness about disabled persons and the need
for integration: "Ten years ago in our part of the world, it was
almost unknown to see disabled persons running their own affairs,
or being very vocal or driving cars ... I think DPI played a major
role."[1]

THE TRINIDAD AND TOBAGO INDEPENDENT LIVING CENTRE

Another achievement of the movement has been the establishment
of the Independent Living Centre (ILC) of Trinidad and Tobago
and the Disabled Women's Network (DAWN T&T), which grew
out of the centre. In August 1988, DPI T&T and the Council of
Canadians with Disabilities (CCD, then known as COPOH) began
discussing independent living concepts.

CCD was founded in 1976 to provide a voice for disabled Canadians, and is composed *of* not *for* disabled persons. It has monitored federal legislation and been successful in obtaining protection for persons with disabilities under the Canadian Charter of Rights and Freedoms and the Canadian Human Rights Act. CCD also has an International Committee with members from across Canada who have an interest in forging solidarity links with their brothers and sisters in developing countries. For several years, CCD had been informing international development agencies in Canada about the need to include disabled persons in their programming.

In 1988, with funds from the Canadian International Development Agency (CIDA), CCD began to send disabled persons to visit its self-help organization counterparts in the Caribbean and to look at ways in which they could exchange information. Francine Arsenault, who was on the CCD board, and Linda Cairns, who was director of an independent living centre in Thunder Bay, Ontario, were sent to Trinidad to explore whether DPI T&T wanted to start an independent living centre. (These centres began to spring up in Canada in the mid-1980s. They are managed by disabled persons and provide information, referrals, needed services and training for disabled persons to live independently in the community.)

In 1990, with support for the idea from DPI T&T, CCD received another grant from CIDA to initiate an independent living centre with DPI T&T in Trinidad. The next three years saw the development of many training programmes in a variety of areas: advocacy, peer counselling, computer literacy, self-esteem, sign language. These courses were met with great enthusiasm and were well attended. The final goal of the courses was to develop trainers within the disabled community to run programmes at the centre.

After two visits to Trinidad, in 1991 and 1992, on behalf of the Council of Canadians with Disabilities, Diane Driedger noted a definite shift in the leadership abilities and involvements of many of the disabled persons she had met two years before: "Many of the participants of the Training for Trainers, peer counselling and advocacy courses told me that they had gained a great deal from the courses ... they had improved their own self-esteem ... People are beginning to say, 'I am somebody and we as disabled persons are somebodies and we demand our rights!' This a change from the past, where many people were worried about ruffling officials if they took a stand on an issue publically."[2]

THE DISABLED WOMEN'S NETWORK OF TRINIDAD AND TOBAGO

As the Independent Living Centre (ILC) was established, disabled women in the organization were beginning to gain a sense that their difficulties were somewhat different from those of men. In 1991, Diane Driedger and Francine Arsenault met with a group of disabled women in Trinidad & Tobago to hear their views. Issues specific to the women were discussed. During Diane's next visit in the fall of 1992, eight women, including Kathleen Guy, met informally. At this meeting, the Disabled Women's Network of Trinidad and Tobago (DAWN T&T) was born. Through publications that CCD had brought to the Caribbean, the women had heard of DisAbled Women's Network Canada (DAWN Canada). They also learned that DAWN Canada and CCD were two separate groups that worked together as part of a greater movement of disability activism. The women liked the name and, with Diane's help, approached DAWN Canada to use the same name. DAWN Canada said that they would be honoured to have their name extended to a sister organization, and DAWN T&T was formed.

At the same meeting in September 1992, a core of six disabled women cited barriers to their integration into society — barriers such as uncooperative families, husbands who kept them shut up in their homes and lack of transportation. This was particularly true for blind women. The group began to strategize about ways to get women out of their homes and into the community. They decided that a woman with a disability should be available at the Independent Living Centre at least once a week to field phone calls from women with disabilities who wished to talk or get information. At the time, only men answered the phones at the centre. The group felt that other women would be more comfortable discussing domestic abuse and other difficult issues with a woman. This 1992 meeting was so exciting because the new DAWN was very dynamic and the women were almost militant in expressing the need for change.

Before the meeting that started DAWN T&T, male members of the ILC had agreed that a female member of the ILC would meet with mainstream women's groups. It was felt that these would be important links for disabled women in Trinidad. The experiences of women with disabilities are the same as those of other women in society, except that their isolation and dependence on the family for income and physical care makes them even more vulnerable. This is why it is important to make all women's resources, such as rape crisis and resource centres, accessible to disabled women.

Kathleen Guy and Diane Driedger were asked by the new DAWN to meet with the Caribbean Association for Feminist Research and Action (CAFRA), which was very receptive to working with DAWN T&T. They said that they had been waiting for disabled women to organize themselves so that the greater women's movement could work directly with disabled women. CAFRA was accessible to mobility-impaired women.

Since its founding in 1992, DAWN T&T has continued to liaise with the women's community. CAFRA has continued to provide needed advice about access to women's services and legal issues. Links have also been made with the Women's Resource Centre in Port of Spain. This centre provides legal advice and training courses in areas such as literacy for women.

DAWN T&T also worked with CAFRA to structure its Voice of Women with Disabilities Poetry Seminar in January 1994. The Seminar was a joint idea of DAWN T&T and CCD. Diane Driedger had contacted MATCH International, a women's development agency in Ottawa, Canada, and suggested that they might be interested in supporting this event, which would also include women from other Eastern Caribbean countries. MATCH funded the event, along with donations from the private sector and individuals in Trinidad, and Diane Driedger spent six weeks in July and August of 1993 mentoring with Kathleen Guy, DAWN T&T's coordinator, at her office in Trinidad. Together, they planned the logistics of running the seminar and visited potential funders and sites.

Several non-disabled CAFRA members served as tutors at the event and it thus became a vehicle for the tutors to learn firsthand about the concerns and abilities of disabled women. As Anselma Mohammed observed in her report, "The retreat was a learning experience for all concerned, as those who were not disabled were given insight into the world of the disabled ... The participants proved to be a very unique and interesting group of people. Even though they were from very diverse backgrounds, they were united in their disability and in their unique appreciation and love for life."[3]

Indeed, as often happens at women-only events, sharing and mutual support, as well as the courses, are very important. Anselma Mohammed reported, "... the deep secrets the participants carried were exposed as they shared in confidence the abuse and emotional pains they had experienced, such as rape, incest and adulterous spouses."[4]

The event reflected the feelings of empowerment that had been present in DAWN T&T from its beginning. As Wendy Edmunds of St. Lucia exclaimed in her report on the workshop, "Each member of the group looked after one another. If anything happened to any member of the group, the other members would 'pitch in' and try to help. I have never come across such a group of loving people. I cannot properly express how I feel about some of them, but I am hoping that in the near future I would be able to write a unique poem on this experience."[5]

In addition to the poetry seminar, DAWN T&T has carried out women's development courses in areas such as self-esteem and everyday living skills in both the north and south of Trinidad. Courses have included dancing lessons and flower arranging. Plans were also made for Judy Croy, a volunteer from the Canadian Executive Services Organization (CESO), to do some management and organizational training with DAWN T&T in 1994 and 1996.

DAWN T&T's other short-term goals are to run an Educational Enhancement Programme, and a Health Maintenance Training Programme to teach disabled women about their bodies, nutrition and sexuality. Often, families neglect training of disabled girls in these areas, thinking that they do not need this knowledge. When this book went to press, DAWN T&T was in the process of becoming an organization independent of DPI T&T, while remaining a member of that group. In the long term, DAWN T&T is looking for some core funding for office operations, which have, for the most part, been run entirely by full-time volunteers — Kathleen Guy, who is the coordinator, and Bill Scott, who is the office assistant. The Global Fund for Women has provided some funding in the past year. Discussions are taking place with various local and Canadian agencies other than CCD. It seems that the process of disabled women coming together in Trinidad and Tobago has not been as easy as was originally thought. It has been a challenge because there are women in Trinidad and Tobago who believe that they ought not get together in groups with other women. It is ironic that men think it natural for women to get together and to talk because it is a practice in Trinidad and Tobago for "the boys" to get together in all kinds of groups, for sports or drinking or just sitting and talking with each other. They regard men getting together as a natural part of life. Many women, though, are suspicious and skeptical of women's groups, not realizing that such groups can be of help in their own lives.

THE IMPACT OF DAWN T&T's WOMEN'S PROGRAMMES ON GENDER RELATIONS

Over the six years that CCD and DPI T&T have been working together, there has been a general openness within DPI T&T to develop programming for women. This goal has been encouraged by several male leaders, who made contacts for Diane Driedger within the mainstream women's movement. At times, however, these same leaders have also handpicked various women they felt should go to meetings with Diane. Sometimes these women, while being competent and well-versed in women's issues, were not in positions within DPI T&T to effect change or to carry through contacts with mainstream women's organizations.

When DAWN T&T was founded and the women's programme was developed, funding went through DPI T&T. This meant that male leaders in the organization had the final say over funding. Thus, women in DAWN T&T had to convince the men of the worthiness of certain expenditures. In contrast, funds granted directly to DAWN were still administered by male staff of DPI T&T, but the women did not need to make the same justifications. This points, perhaps, to an underlying "male control" that still exists within DPI T&T. It is also true that women on the executive and boards of DPI have been loathe to press their own points and to stress points of interest to women.

With the advent of DAWN T&T, these power dynamics have begun to shift. Diane Driedger's visits to DAWN T&T — particularly the six-week trip to work with Kathleen Guy in 1993 — brought home the "seriousness" of DAWN T&T's and CCD's intent to work together on women's issues.

The individual women in DAWN T&T have become more self-assured and more focused about the areas that need to be addressed for the benefit of disabled women. This is partly a result of the meetings and training courses that have already been held by DAWN T&T. The women in DAWN T&T have also learned more about the gender and disability issues that oppress disabled women.

It should be noted that while some male members of the board have joked to Diane Driedger that "You are not interested in the men, you have only come to see the women," there has been a begrudging acceptance that women's concerns are different than men's. Indeed, a small poll of disabled men in the organization, taken by Kathleen Guy, indicated that all of the men said that the women's programme "was needed." She noted that, in general, younger men with disabilities seem more accepting of the notion of women empowering themselves through their own programmes. The men also recognize that women's programming strengthens the overall membership of DPI T&T and enables men and women to work together for changes in society that will benefit all persons with disabilities.

NOTES

1. Rodriguez, Kenwyn, *Equalization of Opportunities: Proceedings of the 3rd World Congress of Disabled Peoples' International, Vancouver, Canada, April 21-26, 1994,* (Winnipeg, Canada: DPI, 1994), p. 62.

2. Driedger, Diane, "COPOH Consultant's Report," unpublished paper, (Winnipeg, Canada, September 1992), p. 1.

3. Mohammed, Anselma, " Voice of Women with Disability Poetry Workshop: An Overview," unpublished article, (Trinidad and Tobago: 1994), p. 3.

4. Ibid.

5. Edmunds, Wendy, "Report on the Workshop for Disabled Women Held in Trinidad," unpublished paper, (St. Lucia: 1994), p. 2.

Kathleen Guy
Interview by Diane Driedger

Putting Faces to Names:
My Visit to Canada, 1995

Women in Canada and in Trinidad and Tobago are interested in improving their lives. Things are different in Canada, in that you have some of the infrastructure in place to do what needs to be done. To me, it seems that women with disabilities in Canada have been working and meeting and advocating for some time, and now they are reaping the rewards of work done before.

Women with disabilities in our two countries both want to work. They want education. They are interested in improving the conditions under which they live. There seem to be problems of abuse in both places. But there are more solutions and options in Canada. Disabled people in Canada seem to want to be totally independent. They want to live on their own. They want to work. People don't seem to be so hooked on wanting to stay in their family homes if there is abuse. If the abuse is happening at home, they can get out by saying: "Let me see if I can get a house or apartment of my own and then maybe this abuse will stop." And the law in Canada — people seem to know their rights! In Canada, people have tested the law and it has worked for a lot of them. There are places they can go to get their problems solved. They can probably call CCD [Council of Canadians with Disabilities], who can hook them up with an agency within the province or city who can help them. CCD can link them to NGOs [non-governmental organizations], church organizations. A lot of people have tested those groups. If they don't work, people seem to know how to ask and demand that they get what is their right.

This is not necessarily true in Trinidad and Tobago. Some people know how to get fair treatment, but a lot of people don't. Some people know and don't do anything about it — they buy into the fact that most people believe that nothing will happen even if they try. For instance, there are services that are available to the general public. They don't test the services to see if they are available to them. I know a woman who had received a cheque from another country and needed to find out if the service that she required to cash the cheque was available to her. She was told that this service was available to the public — so why not you try to see if it is available to you? The person answered, "Because I am a disabled person, I don't think it would be available to me." That was an assumption and it was wrong. The service this woman needed was available to everybody, and if, as a disabled person, that woman had tested it and it didn't work for her, she could have done something about it. If she was in Canada she would have known to say, "Okay, I tested it and I didn't get it done — I can demand that it be done because I am a citizen just like everybody else." A lot of people wouldn't say that at home. They would say, "I didn't get through." Or, now that advocates are around in Trinidad and Tobago, they would say, "You do it for me." We are trying to say, "No, you have to advocate for yourself."

Before I came to Canada, I already had this orientation to help myself. I knew there were things available to people regardless of ability. I mean, maybe I wasn't coming from the kind of background most disabled people are coming from — I was not always disabled — and I was interested in social work and community work, so I knew as a citizen what I was entitled to. When I became a disabled person, I saw some people did not take advantage of things that were available. I would tell people, "You can get that if you ask for it." Some tried and got what they wanted, and now some people know. But it is different coming to Canada and seeing that people actually take it as an everyday occurrence that they have civil rights. And they exercise their rights.

I think I can take back a lot of things from Canada. Some of the things that I've seen here are things that we are doing all the time, but we have not formalized them. I can say to the group, "Let's talk about this and formalize it — they're doing it in Canada and it's called such-and-such." I have seen things that are very high tech that we can use, but we can also work at a lower level. For instance, adapting your house to suit yourself as a disabled person. I've seen people in Winnipeg who have turned their homes into really fine accessible places at low cost. They have invented things by talking about what their needs are. They've worked with people who do not make high tech things. They've talked to mechanics and electricians and different people to get what they need, simply. For instance, we always thought that having a lift was expensive, but after I visited one family's home I realized it doesn't have to be. You can do things with used parts — we are accustomed in Trinidad and Tobago to recycling. We have a lot of inventive and creative people, so we can talk to some of these people and adapt what I've seen.

We tend to have an emphasis on youth in Trinidad and Tobago. Whenever we develop our programmes, we say, "You need the youth." I've learned here that seniors are also contributors. When I say I "learned" it, I really have it in the back of my mind that seniors are usually taxpayers — they are also entitled to have things tailored to their use. I learned that at the ILRC [Independent Living Resource Centre]. I saw it also at the CNIB [Canadian National Institute for the Blind]. At ILRC, I met one person who is in his seventies who did not become an advocate until he was elderly and he's doing a fantastic job. He is one of the most impressive people that I've met here. His disability is severe but he has overcome it by being one of the best volunteers I've seen. He does his work and he is elderly — we don't have to throw away the elderly people. In Trinidad and Tobago, elderly disabled people are not given credit for some of their experiences. There is respect for elderly people but they stay in their homes. In Canada, I see there are institutions that recognize that elderly people have put in some service and some time. The elderly have a place and there are programmes specifically geared to the elderly. Maybe young people don't want to sing the songs of the 1930s and 1940s, but this is something the elderly like to do. There are a lot of places for them to get together and socialize in Canada.

People do not seem to understand the situation in other countries. At one place I visited, the people said, "We have seen your report but now it is so good to see the person." In another place, people were working with Caribbean people and they did not actually know the geographical location of Trinidad and Tobago. Maybe something is missing on our side. Maybe, when we get involved with people, we should tell them exactly where we are. We need to do something about introducing people to how life is where we live. There are some people who do not understand that standards are different in other places but not necessarily lower. In a tropical country, you don't spend a lot of money on clothing — it does not mean the standard of living is lower, it just means that you don't need certain types of clothes. There is no real need for us to spend money on boots. Maybe some people, because they have never been outside of Canada, cannot understand that business and work get conducted in a different way elsewhere. That does not necessarily mean that work does not get done — that it is so laid back or whatever. Also, you take your technology so much for granted and expect that there is technology like that in other places. You take your computers and your fax machines and your Internet, and you figure we have access to the Internet and a computer because we have an office. We do not have the facilities that you have. Something that takes you ten minutes to do may take me two weeks because of the difference in facilities.

Your volunteer system is different from mine, too. Disabled people in Trinidad and Tobago are now just learning to become volunteers. You know about this already. We are still trying to make people accept the fact that the ILC [Independent Living Centre] or DAWN [Disabled Women's Network] will be run by people with disabilities and not necessarily have much need for able-bodied people. We have to tell people in Trinidad and Tobago that. In Canada, I don't think anybody was shocked when I told them that, because you have been doing that for years.

I don't know why Trinidadians have a different view of being volunteers. Quite a few people always want to be paid. Perhaps this is cultural. We have quite a few good volunteers in DAWN now because a lot of people realize that in order to get things done they are probably the ones who have to do it. People are motivated now to be DAWN volunteers because we have a lot of things going on. Once we outline to people what we are doing, they realize they are not just coming to a meeting. If you come this month, you can look forward to doing "such-and-such" next month. There is always something to look forward to. A lot of other organizations have a lot of meetings, but they talk a lot. They say, "We are going to have a walk-a-thon one of these days," and the next week they decide to hold it in November — and November may be a long way away and they talk about it for nine months. We don't do that because we realize that people get tired and it costs them money to come out — a little more money than the average person — and it probably costs a lot of effort to come out. So when they come out they want to have something tangible to show for the time they spent.

I do not know if I have taught anything to anybody here in Canada. In the disability world, it seems that when you can put a face to a name, people work better with one another. But maybe that is not always possible. People here need to know that you can work with people without ever actually seeing them. People need to know more about what others are doing and that they can work together, because all of us can't come to Canada and all of you can't go to Trinidad and Tobago. So we need to find a balance. I think geography is very important, and I think those Canadians who know the geography of the Caribbean owe it to the rest to teach them about it, because I couldn't do a lot of it. But at least I tried.

I came to share — not only to take, but to give. In Trinidad and Tobago, we try to run our group as an organization that gives as well as gets. We don't always take, or always get, get, get. We think that we have something we can share with people. So that is the philosophy that I brought here. I tried to make people see that, if you are working outside your own country, you have to understand where you are working. Once you get to know the people and you understand them, you deal differently with those people.

Judy Heumann

Growing Up: Creating a Movement Together

Those of us who have had disabilities at different life stages have different concerns about risk taking and responsibility. I contracted polio in Brooklyn, New York in 1949, when I was one-and-a-half years old. Because I was disabled early in life, I early on had to face being told that I must fit into a system that frequently does not want me to be there.

In public school, we disabled students learned that we had to believe in ourselves, because the system around us was not set up to help us succeed. If anything, it was set up to help us fail. The teachers did almost everything possible to allow failure to become our reality. When I graduated from the eighth grade, I was the first-ever student from the classes for the disabled to go on to high school. Though the classes had been going on for many years, most of the students had been sent to sheltered workshops after primary school. It was very difficult for those students to ever move beyond the workshops. This was a message which many of us took to heart because we had very strong negative feelings about sheltered workshops. Low self-esteem was, and still is, being reinforced at the workshops through segregation, menial tasks and sub-standard wages.

We also realized very early on that the people working with us — the "professionals" — were not disabled and did not have a strong vested interest in whether or not we made it in life. The teachers never talked about our futures. They never said, "If you want to get a job, you have to work hard in school." They got their paycheque and went home.

In 1969, I graduated from college and decided to become a teacher. But I was not allowed to receive my teaching credentials for the "medical reason" that I had to use a wheelchair. In a well-publicized case, I took on the New York Board of Education and won. Around this time, a friend and I decided that we were going to use my experiences with job discrimination to start an organization. Because of my case with the Board of Education, we were getting hundreds of letters and phone calls from both disabled and non-disabled people; we were often stopped on the street and we were asked to do many TV and radio interviews.

My friend and I were neophytes, but we learned quickly that there were many problems in the world and that it was not just a few of us who thought these problems existed. There were many disabled people who wanted to take control of their lives. They were very angry about the fact that our traditional service organizations were not run by disabled people. The goals of traditional service organizations simply did not reflect how we wanted to shape our lives. So we began to speak out about these problems. If you believe you have nothing to lose, which we did, you can do almost anything — and we *did* do almost anything. We worked on issues regarding transportation and education, and we started to build coalitions among disabled groups. Parents of disabled children became involved, and we also started working with groups that provided services to persons who are mentally handicapped.

I think that the shell we had built around us as disabled people had segregated us from society. We were basically ashamed of who we were. We also knew that if we could not speak out about what was important to us, very little was going to change. It became apparent that we had to make changes occur. The organization we founded as a result of my legal suit, Disabled in Action, still exists in New York, Maryland and Philadelphia, and many of us are proud of our involvement in setting it up. During this time, a huge scandal was uncovered regarding a state school for persons who are mentally handicapped called Willowbrook. We became involved with the organization that had exposed the situation. Our belief that we had nothing to lose made us more combative, and, slowly, we began to change things.

We told people that the goals of service organizations were not what we wanted in our lives. There were no disabled persons on the boards of those organizations and no disabled persons had jobs there. In the 1970s, Disabled in Action tackled issues like transportation and housing, and launched demonstrations.

One of the first major activities of Disabled in Action was a demonstration against President Nixon's veto of the 1972 Rehabilitation Act. The Rehabilitation Act was a symbol for disabled people because it contained provisions for education, independent living, accessibility and anti-discrimination. The veto was a rejection of the wishes of our Congress. During our protest, we were able to temporarily shut down the President's 1972 re-election campaign headquarters in New York City.

We had organized about 50 disabled people to come to our demonstration. In New York there were hardly any private transportation systems and few of us had cars. So we went begging and borrowing just to get transportation to go to the demonstration. Although we did not exactly know what we were going to do, we decided our first step would be to go to the Federal Building.

The Federal Building is on an island in the East River and there is nothing much around it — only a few people on the street and little traffic. But we finally found the building and, eventually, everyone knew we were there. We had brought a coffin with us, and we talked about how the United States Government was trying to kill disabled people. A representative from the Federal Building told us that were not allowed to be there and that he would call the police if we did not leave. When the police arrived, they asked who was responsible for this demonstration. Everybody said that I was.

After this, we decided to move to the Nixon re-election headquarters on Madison Avenue, one of the big thoroughfares in Manhattan. At 4:40 p.m. — during rush hour — we stalled traffic for about 40 minutes and gained some press attention.

Finally, the day before the election, we organized another demonstration, and this time we brought two disabled Vietnam War veterans with us, who got a lot of press coverage in those days. Most of the New York press corps was there. We had a demonstration in Times Square and walked against traffic on Madison Avenue to the Nixon re-election headquarters. We wanted a public debate with President Nixon about why he had vetoed the Rehabilitation Act. Unfortunately, a public debate was not called, but the experience gave us an incredible sense of power. We handed out thousands of flyers on the street, explaining the impact of the veto of the Rehabilitation Act.

The following year, the demonstrations continued full strength, with a march and candlelight vigil in Washington D.C., and we also lobbied in the federal Congress. This time, the act was passed and it included the first civil rights legislation for disabled people, in Section 504; it was comparable to the legislation for people of colour and women.

In 1973, I attended graduate school in Berkeley, California. I also began working with a group called the Centre for Independent Living (CIL). I found it a powerful experience to see severely disabled people live independently in Berkeley, largely as a result of the CIL. Because there was no government paid attendant system (for personal care), I had really been afraid to leave New York, where I had a whole network of friends and relatives helping me. I did not have my own van in New York and so I basically depended on enlisting help from others to get things done. I became a manipulator very early in my life — I think that is a prerequisite for anybody who is disabled. I learned to get as much as I could out of society.

The disabled people in Berkeley seemed to do things differently than we had done in New York. They were dissatisfied with the system and they felt that the professionally run organizations were not meeting their needs. Disabled people were unemployed, disabled people were not board members of service organizations and disabled people were afraid of going back to the institutions that they had just left. The Berkeley organization combined a strong militant advocacy with support services that were not designed to assume the responsibility of government or other non-profit organizations. The fundamental principle of the organization was that it had to be controlled by disabled individuals. For example, paid attendant services had to be controlled by disabled people, and all people could work for the integration of disabled individuals into society, but on disabled people's terms. We wanted to be accepted for what we are — persons with disabilities. For me, integration means having pride, and thus being able to tell people what I need in order to integrate within an organization and into the community and society as a whole.

I am not ashamed of my need to have a group of disabled friends I can go back to regularly. We are willing to support each other. That is what independent living means to me. The Centre for Independent Living, and the more than 150 other independent living programmes in the U.S., are places for disabled people to come for basic assistance in housing, attendant services etc. But, most important, these centres are a powerful voice for integration and equality in our communities.

I gained valuable experiences during my years at Berkeley. I was on the CIL Board of Directors. I also did my Master's programme internship in public health at a Senator's office in Washington and learned how laws and regulations come about. Back in Berkeley, I worked as Chief Deputy Director of the Centre for Independent Living and did programme development serving disabled persons aged twenty and over. At first we were mostly serving people with physical disabilities and people who were blind. Over the years, services were developed for people who were mentally disabled, people who were deaf and people with multiple disabilities.

With the array of new services, the Centre for Independent Living became more diversified and more powerful. Disabled communities began to push hard for change. The concept that we had nothing to lose and everything to gain became stronger and stronger, and more and more changes occurred. Disabled people and some professionals from all over the United States, as well as from other countries, started to come to Berkeley to voice their concerns and to learn firsthand how severely disabled people had changed their lives.

An important milestone in the development of independent living centres was federal legislation which provided programme money within the Rehabilitation Act. The money was a paltry twenty-two million dollars, but it enabled independent living centres to become established throughout the United States. Most of the centres strongly support the philosophy of control by disabled people. Their core services include information and referral, and attendant care services. (There is no national attendant service in the U.S.; provision of attendant services is left to the discretion of the different states.) The disabled person hires, fires and trains the attendant but the centre does the first screening. Thus, disabled persons have control over who they would like to provide their attendant care, and over how it is done.

Peer support is a fundamental part of Independent Living Centres — disabled people working with other disabled people in peer-counselling relationships. It helps disabled people to realize that other people have been through the same experiences and that together they can work on getting on with life. Some of the centres provide job placement services and other services for a wide range of disability groups — for example, the Berkeley Centre now serves people with all types of disabilities. The fundamental goal of the Berkeley Centre is to open its doors to all people who want to participate, and to create access for disabled people to the benefits of society.

The independent living movement subscribes to the philosophy that disabled people must have respect for themselves, that they know what is right for them, that they must have the ability to say "no" and that they can develop the ability to turn power around and manage it themselves. To me, independent living is: power, self-respect, the belief that we can make a difference and the ability to make that difference through an international alliance of all disabled people. Today, we see the independent living movement flourishing throughout the world, in countries such as Canada, Germany, Sweden, Italy, Mexico, Nicaragua and Japan. We are disabled people articulating our needs and fighting for the right to be equal members of our communities. We have so much still to accomplish, but we can be proud of the changes we have been initiating throughout the world. Today, we are overcoming.

Snapshot from Beijing
Interview by E. Catherine Boldt

Judi Rogers
Through the Looking Glass, United States

I wanted to come to Beijing for several reasons. One, to show China that women with disabilities can be productive. I also wanted to show other women with disabilities that they can pursue their dreams to become pregnant and build equipment that makes parenting easier and successful. In addition, being a breast cancer survivor, I wanted to bring up those issues, because some women are unable to do a monthly exam and I think that, right now, that is the only safe way to detect it. Mammograms have 10 percent to 40 percent false negatives. My cancer was missed for many, many years even though I had a mammogram once a year. So I wanted to bring this message: I would like women to get their health centres to provide monthly exams for those who are unable to do self-exams.

My philosophy became more specific after the breast cancer. I realized life is filled with speed bumps and it's all in how you get over them. So, basically, you have to say: "This, too, I can handle." I'm determined to do something that I think is important. I try — not always successfully — not to get overwhelmed. Sometimes, the situation here [in Beijing] has pushed me to the edge and I have screamed and I have become the ugly American by pounding my fist on the table and screaming, "No!" And they look at me in a very shocked, chagrined way!

Pat Danforth, *Canada*

just me

sometimes in the cool dark i dream of what can be
shaped by the past
shaped by the crash
i cry out in silence and say
can't you see
i'm just me
riding around in a chair but still just me
don't put your values on my body
don't say i'm brave
don't say i'm noble
realize i'm just me, not better not worse, just me

Pat Danforth, *Canada*

i said, he said

i said, tell me about your dreams and desires
he said, so, how long have you been in a chair
so, i told him

i said, i'm new, i just started using wheels
he said, so, you want to be taken care of
so, i let him take care of me

i said, i've never been with a man since i broke my back
he said, so, you want to have sex
so, we had sex

i said, do you want to live together
he said, so, you want to get married
so, we got married

i said, let's talk about having a family
he said, so, you want to have a baby
so, i had a baby

i said, let's talk about caring for our son
he said, so, you want a baby-sitter
so, i got a baby-sitter

i said, let's talk about my going back to work
he said, so, you want to get a job
so, i got a job

i said, let's talk about my job offer in edmonton
he said, so, you're moving to edmonton
so, we moved to edmonton

i said, let's talk about you getting a job, it's been 6 months
he said, so, teaching jobs are hard to find
so, he sold merchandise

i said, let's talk about my job offer in regina
he said, so, you're moving to regina
so, we moved to regina

i said, let's talk about you finding a job, it's been 8 months
he said, so, jobs are hard to find
so, he sold merchandise

i said, let's talk about what you really want
he said, so, you want me to take the teaching job
so, he taught

i said, let's talk about the future
he said, so, i never thought i'd stay with you
so, i cried

i said, let's talk
he said, so, you always tell me what to do
so, he left

i said, is there someone else
he said, so, you don't trust me
so, i learned not to trust him

i said, do you want to work on the relationship
he said, so, you're having a problem
so, i went to counselling

i said, let's talk about child support
he said, so, i have no money
so, he pays child support

i said, let's talk about divorce
he said, so, you can't have the house
so, i have the house

i said, let's talk about the time you spend with your son
he said, so, i spend enough time
so, my son seldom sees him

i said, i don't need to talk to you
he said, so
so

Snapshot from Beijing
Interview by E. Catherine Boldt

Kim Mi Yeon
*Research and Institute of the Differently Abled,
Seoul, South Korea*

I am a 28-year-old woman. I grew up in a good family. My father has a drugstore. I have two brothers. My family doesn't consider me a disabled person, so I had a good education and went to university.

Last year I met my husband. He was a cook in a hotel. The interesting thing is that I am a nutritionist! When he saw me for the first time, I was sitting on a chair so he didn't know I am a woman with a disability. After that meeting, I stood up with difficulty. He was so surprised and disappointed. At the time, I didn't know him.

After a year, he came to me and said to me, " I want to date you, but you are a handicapped woman, I could not exactly contact you." In South Korea, they think disabled women cannot work in the house, cannot take care of their family. So he was also very worried about that. So, after the first date — seven months later — we were married.

In South Korea, the man doesn't work in the house. But my husband has to do many things. That is uncomfortable for him because, when he was growing up and he lived with his family, he didn't do anything. But he had to do everything after our marriage. So we have to talk to each other.

Nuggehalli Sitaram Hema

Hopes and Dreams: The Situation for Women with Disabilities in India

INTRODUCTION

I begin with a quote attributed to an ancient Lawmaker of India named Manu, who is known for his treatise on women and their role in family and society, written in 200 BC: "In childhood a woman must be subject to her father, in youth to her husband and when her Lord is dead, to her son. A woman must never be independent."

We have come a long way from there! That is evident particularly in the fact that, in the fall of 1995, so many of us Indian women travelled all the way to the Fourth World Conference on Women in China, to address issues that affect us.

Yet thousands of women from India, particularly in rural India, lead an existence of extreme subservience, with very little control over their lives. Women with disabilities suffer not only the usual discrimination against females, but also are further discriminated against because of their disabilities. This double prejudice, compounded

98

by illiteracy and superstition, makes women with disabilities one of the most disadvantaged groups in the world.

Although, overtly, the situation today appears bleak, changes are occurring — even if at a very slow pace. A number of women with disabilities have overcome prejudice and negative social attitudes to become role models to others. Having realized this, some non-governmental organizations (NGOs) have taken up these issues and are working towards enriching alternatives. Over the years, the Indian government has also formulated some excellent policies to address issues affecting persons with disabilities such as health care, rehabilitation, education, training etc.

How many of these policies and alternatives actually reach those for whom they are intended? To find this out, and also to explore the significance of "gender and disability" in the lives of Indian women with disabilities, we met and spoke to a number of such women at the Association of the Physically Handicapped (APH) in Bangalore City.

Bangalore has a population of six million, and is located in the State of Karnataka in Southern India. APH was formed there in 1959, to show that people with disabilities could become active contributors to society. Today, APH is involved in many activities, all based on the following goals: to meet individual needs; to create awareness; to promote acceptance and integration; to instill self-confidence; and to encourage self-reliance for the benefit of persons with disabilities.

The women we interviewed were between 18 and 60 years of age, had different types and levels of disabilities and also came from varying socio-economic and educational backgrounds. Some of them had lived in Bangalore all their lives, some had come from bigger or smaller towns, some from rural areas and some others had lived in institutions for girls and women. Our interactions with the women included group discussions, interviews, informal chats and questionnaires. Many of them were candid and clear in voicing their points of view regarding several issues that affected their lives. The group discussions were particularly stimulating — participants were alternately analytical and objective, pensive and, sometimes, humorous in getting their points across in an emotionally loaded atmosphere. Through it all, there was always the question: "Why should it be so for me?"

These women with disabilities have their ideas and their hopes about how to make their lives more meaningful. Let me share with you what we learned from all of them about their life situations — situations which reflect, at a micro-level, the overall situation for the Indian woman with a disability.

ACCESS TO HEALTH CARE AND REHABILITATION

Ideally, health care and rehabilitation should mean an entire process that starts with the identification of the individual with special needs and initial assessments, and then works out appropriate individual programmes for economic, intellectual and emotional development. Among the women we met, very few had had sustained access through all these stages of care and rehabilitation, particularly in their early years.

Any rehabilitation work in the field of disabilities would be rendered meaningless if the preventative aspect is ignored. Hence the Government of India (aided by voluntary organizations, both Indian and international) has launched major immunization programmes. In spite of these programmes, which have made a tremendous impact all over the country, there still exists a very large percentage of children (particularly in rural areas) who are not immunized, due to parental ignorance regarding the programme or lack of access to government facilities for immunization or superstitious beliefs and fears about immunization itself. As a result, rarely but shockingly, some children still develop polio. In recent years, the Indian government has launched intensive awareness and motivation campaigns for vaccination.

After the onset of disability, for a vast number of families — even those in urban areas — health care consists mainly of visits to doctors (often several doctors), which results in medical advice only. This advice is sadly and all too frequently inadequate or, worse, inaccurate. The result is the loss of precious time before the start of interventions such as suitable surgery, therapy, aids etc. Timely references to appropriate rehabilitation organizations are very rare. Even if they do manage to get to such an organization, the family is frequently unable to meet the cost of using even subsidized services, and this, together with poor transportation facilities, makes regular visits to these organizations very difficult. Sporadic visits make the intervention programme ineffective. Hence even these limited facilities are being utilized only by a microscopic few. From the statistics available, it can be inferred that, in India, there are about 20 million girls and women with disabilities. This gives us an idea of the magnitude of the problem. Less than one percent of women with disabilities can avail themselves of the existing facilities, which are provided mainly by NGOs.

In this dismal picture, it is the NGOs that are the proverbial "silver lining." Many NGOs (including our own organization, APH) find the Community Based Rehabilitation (CBR) approach practical and workable in addressing the issues of women with disabilities. This is because such an approach makes it possible to bring about changes within the traditional systems, where the woman's health needs were relegated to last place in a hierarchy of family needs. Over a period of time, through broad-based spectrum health programmes which cover physical and medical rehabilitation, general health, nutrition, health awareness etc., the NGOs have managed to bring about changes within whole communities — changes in outlook, perception and attitudes towards gender and disability.

EDUCATION, VOCATIONAL TRAINING AND EMPLOYMENT

It has said by no less a person than Ralph Waldo Emerson that, "The secret of education lies in respecting the pupil." Well, "respect" is a concept we, in India, know and understand. We respect our parents, our elders, our teachers! A woman is revered as a mother (particularly if she bears sons) or if she is old enough to be an "elder." So where does that leave a young woman who is disabled? By these standards, hardly worthy of respect!

In the conservative sectors of our society — where education and training are seen solely as an investment in breadwinners — the education of women is considered a frivolous luxury. So it is hardly surprising that, in the majority of families, educating a woman with a disability is considered quite unnecessary.

Here again it is the NGOs, working in rural, semi-urban and urban communities, that have brought about drastic changes in the lives of women. It is through their efforts that the women (able-bodied or disabled) in these communities are being seen as target groups for educational and training programmes. Government endorsement of these programmes, through the introduction of new policies and programmes for women based on recommendations made by NGOs, help in giving women with disabilities better access to existing government and NGO facilities or programmes for education, training, income generation and awareness.

The significance of these interventions by NGOs can be seen from the experiences of one group of women with visual impairment. The five women in the group come from families residing in rural areas of Karnataka State. In their villages, their gender and disability, together with their families' illiteracy, worked completely against them. Their families and communities never expected anything worthwhile from them, and attitudes towards them were totally negative and discouraging. The entry of NGOs into their communities was really instrumental in rehabilitating them in different ways. The organizations convinced their families of the need to do something to help them and also provided facilities for this. The women considered it a breakthrough that their families' attitudes had changed from being extremely negative to beginning to be positive.

Today, the five women have chosen to live independently, away from their families (although they visit them from time to time). Four of these women live in a hostel in Bangalore City run by an organization working for the visually impaired. Three of them are employed in the State Government's Telecommunications Department while the fourth works with the State Government's Weaving Board. The fifth woman, I am proud to say, has been trained and employed by our organization as a physiotherapist. She lives with her husband, who is also visually impaired.

We are aware that, in India, only a small percentage of women with disabilities are economically independent. However, the NGOs are now making concentrated efforts to identify the abilities of women with disabilities and match them with the resources available. Women with disabilities are now being trained in skills and professions which provide better income-generating prospects, as well as more intellectual stimulation, than earlier training in tailoring, basket weaving etc. (which have been the stereotypical training areas for all persons with disabilities). Women with disabilities are enrolling themselves in training courses in general electronics, electronics assembling, draughtsman and mechanical training, assembly line operations, telecommunications, cooking and management of professional catering services etc. Many women with disabilities have also entered the disability rehabilitation field as professional social workers, counsellors, village and community level workers etc. In metropolitan cities like Bombay, Delhi and Bangalore, they have trained and have found employment in the more dynamic fields of computers, communications, journalism etc. A strong focus is now also being put on self-employment and enterprise development and financial institutions are also coming forward to assist such schemes. Sometimes the NGOs' sustained and dogged efforts have brought on uniquely positive results, where a female child with a disability is actually more educated than her able-bodied siblings — even male siblings.

RELATIONSHIP WITH FAMILIES OR CARE-GIVERS

Pushpa used to be an intelligent, energetic and happy young woman of twenty-three. She comes from a fairly well-educated middle class family and was working as a secretary in a private firm. Life was good — until the day of Pushpa's accident. It was an accident which, in a single moment, transformed her into a woman with profound disabilities completely dependent on others and unable to speak beyond a few whispered words. Her family placed her in an institution.

Human relationships the world over are extremely complex. Among the most intense, dynamic and perhaps most perplexing are those that exist within families and between family members. The families of women with disabilities are no different. Perhaps because of the existence of the disability and the ensuing interactions with professionals, these families come under closer scrutiny. What, then, is the family's role in providing care for the day-to-day existence of women with disabilities? Does their role extend beyond meeting everyday requirements and needs and stretch into investing for the future?

Despite urbanization and the increasing number of nuclear families in the cities, most Indian families still provide a secure, strong
and loving base where the individual is nurtured. Families, each
within their means, rarely fall short when it comes to providing
physical care, love and affection. Providing for food, clothing and
shelter are functions taken on — in most cases — by the families of
women with disabilities. The actual physical care and assistance
required by some women with disabilities are, generally, attended to
by the mother or an older female sibling. Among better-off families,
hired helpers attend to the day-to-day assistance, generally under
supervision. In a few families where the means are available, financial
and security provisions are made for the woman with disabilities,
usually through lump sum monetary deposits. These provide a house
etc. to ensure a comfortable life for the woman in the future.

For women living in institutions, however, the institutionaliza-
tion was necessary because their basic requirements were not
fulfilled at home. Their families either could not or, in some cases,
sadly, would not care for them.

Families' contributions to the well-being of women with disabilities go well beyond merely providing assistance and being care-giv-
ers. They play a major role, through their actions, attitudes and
values, in the way a woman with a disability looks at herself, and
what she aspires to and expects of herself. A majority of women
with disabilities admit to feeling stifled by what they perceive as
over-concern and over-protection from their families, however
well-intentioned these concerns might be. They acknowledge the
fact that, by venturing out alone, they could become easy targets.
They also appreciate their family's anxiety about their safety.
However, is being confined to protected areas the answer? Given
the chance, do we not have the capacity and intelligence to learn to
cope?

Another feature of familial ties is that of adjustment and compro-
mise. It has been part of Indian tradition (sometimes mistakenly
called, "culture"), for women to make all the adjustments — so
much so that families take this for granted. Women with disabilities
have an added feeling of indebtedness for all the physical assistance
they receive. This feeling is so intense and ever-present — even when
family relationships are warm and spontaneous — that women with
disabilities would endure and suffer silently any amount of discomfort

and pain rather than express their needs and requirements, lest they add to their families' burdens.

Physical assistance for the woman with disabilities is generally provided to the best of each family's capacity. It is the emotional aspect — the support and understanding of emotional needs — that we need to examine. Emotional support from families often means protecting the woman with disabilities from harsh realities, trying to make her feel secure, and just being there. When it comes to more subtle forms of support — like bridging an emotional void or resolving emotional conflicts or just overcoming a sudden feeling of dejection and hopelessness — very few families seem to be able to handle these complex issues. Sensitivity to this need, of course, varies greatly among families. Lots of families just do not acknowledge the existence of feelings and emotions of this nature in women, particularly when they are disabled. However, a large number of families are acutely aware and deeply sensitive to this aspect in their daughter's or sister's life but are unable to handle it.

Most women with disabilities have had to find their own ways of coping. Some open up to friends who may be similarly disabled, others write out their feelings in private, some find solace in prayers and still others develop hobbies and other interests so as not to get weighed down by their feelings. However, this appears to be an area where both the women and their families are still seeking answers. The professional counselling available in most organizations does not seem to provide a suitable alternative or even begin to fill the gap.

Perhaps relationships with other disabled or able-bodied individuals or groups that can provide the opportunity for catharsis and empathetic listening is part of the answer. Also, opportunities to meet other women who have been through similar or more difficult experiences, and have coped in a positive manner, could help. Meeting such individuals may give parents, too, new insights into their own disabled daughters' situation. Almost every woman we spoke to endorsed our own conviction that, given proper, all-round awareness regarding disability, the family is the best unit for care, growth and fulfilment.

PARTICIPATION IN COMMUNITY LIFE

Vasanthi, who is orthopaedically disabled and has a diminutive stature, has four sisters. In spite of being completely independent physically, she did not attend any of her sisters' marriages. Her parents insisted each time that she stay back, as they said that the journey and the function would tire her. It is obvious that they did not want her to be seen for fear of deterring prospective and future marriage alliances for her remaining sisters.

Two important factors play a significant role in a disabled woman's ability, or lack of ability, to participate in community life. The first factor is physical — in other words, whether the nature and the level of a woman's disability, combined with the structural and architectural designs in her environment, make it possible for her to venture outside her home without too much difficulty. The second factor is social: How do people in her family and community view her disability?

In order to tackle the physical aspect of community participation, NGOs in disability rehabilitation are striving hard to provide more and more mobility aids and to make these as individualized and cost-effective as possible. Attempts are also being made to widen the distribution network for these aids.

As for "structural adjustments" in public places, the remark of one of our group participants seems to say it all: "In India, this is just not an issue at all." In Indian cities, when we speak of physical impediments in the "outside world," we are talking about things like crowded streets, overflowing buses, hostile bus conductors, unwilling autorickshaw drivers, bumpy roads, the jeering public and an occasional concerned citizen who says, in a sympathetic tone, "Why do you need to travel like this? Better stay at home!" In public buildings, often the available alternatives are long flights of stairs or lifts which, at most times, do not function. When they do, in all probability they are not big enough to accommodate a wheelchair! Faced with such situations, the idea of modifying facilities to aid mobility and access in public places appears impossible and far-fetched. Still, activists in the field are raising their voices to at least have this issue recognized and acknowledged.

Generalizations about social attitudes to disability, particularly in recent times, are not always accurate. Attitudes can vary from being extremely negative to totally positive. Rural families are generally more tolerant of individual differences and, unless a woman is very severely disabled, she is able to merge into the family routine and household chores. However, social perceptions and superstitions can greatly hinder the disabled woman's attempts to fully integrate into society. Superstition plays a significant role in keeping the woman with disabilities hidden away in both rural and urban settings. Considering the presence of a woman with a disability to be inauspicious during important events, or believing that her presence may come in the way of marriage prospects for other female siblings, adds to the isolation and loneliness of women with disabilities.

In such situations, one successful strategy adopted by NGOs is to identify achievers among women with disabilities from the community and involve them in the organization's work. This not only necessitates that these women go around in their communities and be visible, it also presents them, subtly, as role models. This enhanced role, when taken on by the disabled woman, has made her family and her community look at her anew. They begin to see a "person with abilities," not a "woman with a disability."

In recent years, the media has also been used to project the positive aspects of persons with disabilities, thus bringing about changes in the community. It is hoped that, in the long run, this will motivate and promote other women with disabilities to participate at all levels and in all kinds of work and social situations.

MARRIAGES AND MARITAL RELATIONSHIPS

When the issue of marriage was introduced during our group sessions, there was complete silence for a moment. This, in itself, signifies the intense conflicts that the issue of marriage raises in women with disabilities.

In India, where arranged marriages are still the norm, women with disabilities are at a disadvantage. The disadvantage is due mainly to societal definitions of, and expectations from, marriage. In rural communities and among the urban lower-middle-class and poorer families, the wife is expected to do a lot of physical labour.

When a marriage alliance is negotiated between two such families, the presence, nature and the level of physical disability of the prospective bride assumes importance. This approach to assessment of marital attributes has had its impact on women with disabilities themselves. Women with hearing impairments or marginal orthopaedic disability or even (to a lesser extent) visual impairments consider themselves to have better chances of marriage than women with severe orthopaedic disabilities or cerebral palsy.

Societal perception of marriage as the final responsibility of the parents toward their daughters leads some families to resort to any means, fair or foul, to find them husbands. Instances of women with disabilities being married off to already married men are many. In the north Indian States like Haryana, Punjab and Rajasthan, it is not uncommon for two sisters, one able-bodied and one disabled, to be married to the same man. After all, this enables parents literally to kill two birds with one stone!

Among urban, educated, upper-middle-class families, a woman's physical appearance, educational and other accomplishments are considered so important that the woman who is disabled is made to feel inadequate and unsuitable for marriage. Her own family perpetuates such values, and reacts with panic and vehement disapproval should she express her desire to marry and set up a home. But when it is the man who has the disability, then things are not quite so tough. There are many parents who are willing to give their able-bodied daughters in marriage to him!

Families of disabled women — and the women themselves — have many fears and anxieties associated with marriage and its implications. Often, these are based on observations about the perceived marital relationships of others rather than on firsthand experience. They fear that the woman will experience harassment and abuse after marriage. Frequent media reports of such abuse and ill-treatment by the husband and in-laws reinforces such fears.

The biggest underlying fear, though, is that the disabled woman will be deserted by an able-bodied husband. This is not so difficult to understand, as desertion of the wife — able-bodied or disabled — is a very common occurrence in India, particularly among the poorer families. But what makes it different in this context is that many disabled women see desertion as further proof of their own inadequacy. It would seem to me that being deserted by an unsympathetic husband is, relatively speaking, a preferable fate to that of one woman whom we spoke to, whose husband, while living with her, disregarded her feelings and emotions utterly. She was in an accident and became disabled 40 days after her marriage. Her husband's rejection of her is total and he is bent upon marrying again. If fate had willed otherwise and it was her husband who had become disabled, would the wife think of leaving him and marrying again? In all probability, she would have spent the rest of her life looking after his needs.

Inaccurate, preconceived ideas about a disabled woman's ability to care for her children are often quoted as reasons for her to remain single. These ideas persist even among disabled women themselves, leading them to question their own worth and capacity for parenthood. Such notions about child care are related to traditional views of parental roles within marriage, where the mother is the only, or, at least, the primary parent. Bringing up children is considered to be mainly her responsibility.

A crucial aspect of marriage is the sexual relationship between husband and wife. Raising the issue in the context of marriage for women with disabilities generates feelings of acute discomfort. We have not been able to discuss this issue openly. There is much mis-information, and many misconceptions, about sexuality and sexual relationships, which are further perpetuated by the media and works of popular romantic fiction. At present, our attempts to tackle this issue are at best tentative and cursory.

Does all this mean happy marriages are non-existent among women and men who are disabled? Of course not! Happy marital unions do exist, where the relationships have grown and matured to such an extent that the disability of a spouse is not an issue at all.

Nagrathnamma's life is a happy illustration of such a union. Born with total visual disability, she has been married to her abled-bodied husband for over fifteen years. She has two older children. She shares a warm, happy relationship with her husband and her children. All four of them share responsibilities when it comes to managing the household. She says she is blessed with a wonderful husband and is totally content with her lot in life!

Fears and anxieties related to marriage are so strong that women with disabilities believe them to be the whole truth. Failed marriages seem to be taken as the universal norm — so much so that many of the women prefer to remain single rather than take the plunge and risk rejection and hurt. Because of their fears, they look upon economic independence as an alternative to the security marriage is supposed to provide rather than a statement about their own capabilities. All these fears and anxieties notwithstanding, a majority of the women with disabilities we spoke to openly acknowledged their desire for marriage and an emotionally fulfilling marital relationship. At the same time, they are very clear about the importance of being economically independent. They have shown increased self-esteem and confidence and are able to place marriage and their individual identities in proper perspectives.

CONCLUSION

The development of women in India has definitely become a publicly acknowledged issue which politicians or governments can no longer afford to ignore. Thanks largely to the committed efforts of the NGOs, this development has now touched the lives of women with disabilities. They have been shown a way out of an isolated, lonely, passive existence, through education, employment and economic independence. They are becoming empowered. They have choices. They can now hope and dream.

> "I prefer to be a dreamer among the humblest with visions to be realized, than Lord among those without dreams and desires."
> — *Kahlil Gibran*

Snapshot from Beijing
Interview by E. Catherine Boldt

Yuhanis Adnan
Malaysian Spinal Injury Organization

I'm into sports. Back home in Malaysia, we're trying to form a new sport and fitness organization for women with disabilities. So, we are forming that and I am in charge of it.

I am an outgoing person, and back in Malaysia, some disabled persons are still in their shelters. They don't want to go out. I'm trying to reach out: "Hey look at me, I can do this." It's kind of frustrating. I was thinking that, with developing countries here, I would like to exchange information on how to reach out to them. I think that's the most important thing.

In Malaysia, those with disability — maybe it's the culture or attitude — have a stigma: "You are disabled, you should stay at home and just be there." [Most disabled people] are put into a shelter and do all those vocational things. They'll be lucky if, by the time they go out, they can find some work, plus have some financial back-up. And that's why I think it leads to them not coming out from the shelter. Probably they are in their comfort zone. They say: "I am disabled, I shouldn't go out."

Compared to the men, the women's voice in Malaysia is louder. They [the women] have been doing this lobbying — those who are educated, those who went abroad and came back. But those who have been in Malaysia, they still keep to themselves. That's a problem. We've tried to reach out, but maybe our strategy is not appropriate. [People think that,] being disabled, we should withdraw from society. This thought should be changed. We can contribute to society, given a chance.

I always take things as a challenge. When I was told I was confined to a wheelchair, well, that's another challenge. I just go on. Life goes on and I make the best out of it. That's my motto.

Cathy Lysack

Disability and *Gotong-Royung*: The Experience of Women in Indonesia with Community Based Rehabilitation

INTRODUCTION

Gotong-Royung *is the Bahasa Indonesian word for mutual self-help. When the ideal of* gotong-royung *is achieved, women with disabilities in Indonesia will have hope.*

My first real contact with disability and disabled persons came during my training as an occupational therapist in Canada. At the beginning of this training, I recall having two distinctly uncomfortable feelings: first, that I would never remember all the medical information I believed essential to a therapist's success; and, second, that it would be terribly presumptuous to believe I could judge what disabled persons might need. Thus began my search for the meaning of disability from the perspective of disabled people. I became a student of the disability movement and people with disabilities became my teachers. One of my many privileges during this journey has been the opportunity to study disability in countries like Indonesia, where Community Based Rehabilitation (CBR) and mutual support have greatly enhanced the lives of many disabled women.

The two stories that follow illustrate the situation of women with disabilities in Indonesia and the effects that Community Based Rehabilitation had on their lives. These stories are "blended vignettes" from my field research conducted in Central Java in 1990. Names, dates and places have been changed to protect these women, but the events described really happened. The challenges the women confronted were real. The strategies they came up with to overcome their disadvantage bear testimony to their personal courage *and* the value of the mutual support of other women.

PARWATI'S STORY

Parwati was eight years old when she got polio. The epidemic moved quickly through her small village and her older sister died, like several others in Sukoharjo. Both of Parwati's legs were severely affected and it was five months before she was able to move them, although even then she was not able to move them enough to be able to walk. While Parwati tried to get stronger, she remained at home with her mother. She saw her two younger brothers go to school, play with friends and help their father harvest cloves. Parwati stopped going to school because she could not walk the three kilometres there and back. For the next seven years, she lived at home and her parents tried to find ways for her to contribute to the family's welfare.

> *My mother ... she kept me as part of the family. I could not go anywhere but lived in the house, depending on my parents for food, water, caring and everything for life. I crawled on hands and knees in order to move around in the house and in the area where we lived.*

Parwati was kept busy with the family's laundry and cooking. Every second day, her mother carried water up the hill from the nearby river so that Parwati could do the household tasks. In the first year of her polio, Parwati's father fashioned a simple wagon so he could bring Parwati to visit their relatives. As she got older, she was too heavy, it took too long and her father did not like the rest of the village to see her this way. When she was first sick with polio, Parwati wanted to see her friends and missed them deeply. By the time she was 15 years old, she was embarrassed about her appearance. Her legs were withered and permanently bent. Her parents worried greatly about her future. Who would want to marry a girl who could not walk and perform all the daily tasks a wife and young mother ought to perform?

This is the situation that greeted Waktu, a Community Based Rehabilitation (CBR) cadre, on her first visit to Sukoharjo village. Waktu was from the CBR Centre in Solo. It was there that, two years earlier, she had been trained to recognize disabilities and promote positive attitudes toward disabled persons, and had learned how to assist families to develop skills to help their disabled family members. Waktu had seen the results of polio before, and she also had a daughter who had badly broken her leg after falling from a tree. Although the daughter's leg was deformed, she could walk. Waktu understood Parwati's parents' fears. It took many visits and talks with Parwati and her family to convince them that polio was not caused by past family misdeeds. It also took time to convince the family that Parwati should learn new skills to help her earn a living, even if this was unlikely to provide sufficient funds to buy a special wheelchair. Everyone who had visited the family before Waktu had talked about how sorry they were for Parwati. No one, until Waktu, had even asked what Parwati wanted and liked to do.

Parwati loved the beautiful batik her mother would dye and weave into fabric for sarongs. Waktu cajoled a friend, a seamstress, to take Parwati two days a week to learn the trade. The seamstress was skeptical at first, but finally agreed to take Parwati as an apprentice, and Parwati did succeed. Fortunately, she learned quickly and the seamstress had plenty of work. Over the next three years, Parwati's skills developed appreciably. Her income was steady — just over half as much as her father's. Today, Parwati is still not married but she has money for herself and meets many people. She is happier and now feels she can make a real contribution to her community.

... now I see everyone in the village — everyday someone new, people I hardly remember from when I was a baby. I belong with them. I love the busy market and to watch so many people! I feel more accepted now. Sometimes they don't understand, but I know my life is better.

DIAH'S STORY

Diah was just twenty and expecting her first child when she had a bad accident — spilling hot cooking oil — that badly burned her arms and chest. The event was traumatic and Diah had to overcome many difficulties. The injury left the muscles and skin on Diah's arms very scarred and contracted. She had some difficulty lifting pots and carrying her babies, but she found another way to do most work. Today, at age fifty, Diah can reflect on her life and take pride in raising her seven children. Her youngest son is still at home with Diah and her husband Sumadi, a school teacher, but the others are married and have growing families of their own.

Diah is an active woman in her village of Pacitan, but she can easily recall that moment 30 years ago when she feared, albeit briefly, a divorce from her husband and felt great concern about how to care for the baby who would soon arrive. Diah was fortunate that Sumadi was a loving husband who cared deeply for his wife — the accident did nothing to diminish his affection. Diah and Sumadi knew a woman, however, whose husband often mistreated her. They expected any day to hear him shout *talak* three times to divorce her. When that day came, they knew she would be without property, with no means of support and likely without her children, too. They spoke of Diah's accident only rarely, but both knew that Diah's fate might have been different.

Diah had always been a strong student and Sumadi had encouraged Diah to continue her schooling while they awaited the arrival of their first child. Diah had completed her examinations for university entrance but decided not to go when she discovered she was pregnant. That was when she was burned. At the time of Diah's accident, there were no rehabilitation services in Pacitan. After one week in hospital, she returned home and tried her best to manage. Her mother's help was invaluable, especially when the babies were small.

Thirty years later, much has changed. Just recently, health workers visited Diah and Sumadi at their home. They were conducting a door-to-door survey for disability. They were very interested in Diah's experience and convinced her to attend an information meeting in Pacitan to discuss Community Based Rehabilitation (CBR). Diah was recruited to be a CBR worker at that meeting. She was willing to volunteer, and the others at the meeting encouraged her, saying her patience and self-determination were a good example to others. They also knew she was smart, skillful, dedicated and very kind-hearted — just the qualities they believed necessary for a good CBR cadre. Today, Diah is a committed CBR cadre. She has travelled to Leksono, Wonosobo and Sojokerto, telling mothers about her accident and what might have happened if her family had not been supportive. Diah's experience encouraged other mothers to look positively at the abilities of their children and think creatively about how to build bamboo walkers to help them walk or how to give them simple chores in the house just like their other brothers and sisters. After her training at the Solo CBR Centre, Diah was also very good at providing school teachers with ideas about how to involve disabled children in their classrooms. From Diah's point of view, it is mostly a positive attitude and willingness to learn that makes the greatest difference in improving the lives of disabled people.

DISABILITY IN INDONESIA

To be disabled in a developing country means that, in all likelihood, you will receive no professional rehabilitation services in your lifetime.[1] To be a disabled woman means that even your chances of survival are lowered. It is more dificult to address the needs of disabled persons through the national system of health services in Indonesia because of the challenges posed by natural geography and the limited professional and financial resources for health.

Indonesia is a country of nearly 190 million people. It is a huge archipelago in Southeast Asia made up of nearly 14,000 islands that cover more than 15,000 kilometres. One doctor and three nurses are responsible for the health of about 40,000 people. People get medical help at the *puskesmas* (district health centres), which can be between two and twenty-five kilometres from their homes. More meaningful contact with the community may be made at the *posyandus* (village health posts), however. Local villagers take turns volunteering at local health posts. Hence, it is at the *posyandus* that relationships of trust and mutual support can develop. By linking to *posyandus*, community based disability projects have the greatest chance of success.

THE CBR DEVELOPMENT AND TRAINING CENTRE IN SOLO

Parwati's and Diah's stories are like those of other women in Central Java who have been reached by Community Based Rehabilitation. Their stories show that, when disabled women are supported, they can make a difference in the lives of others. The projects of Professor Dr. Soeharso at the CBR Development and Training Centre in Solo, Indonesia, which have similar goals, are also successful. This non-governmental organization supports disabled people, including women, in their communities and strives to improve their lives through CBR. The Solo CBR Centre is one branch of the Yayasaan Pembinaan Anak Cacat (YPAC, or the Indonesian Society for the Care of Disabled Children). Located in Solo, Central Java, the Centre trains CBR workers — called cadres — to identify community disability priorities and help start community action.

Although CBR training includes identifying disabilities and simple rehabilitation measures, it also emphasizes promoting positive attitudes towards disabled persons and coming up with creative ideas for disabled persons' participation in the community. The ultimate goal is a better quality of life and meaningful, social involvement in one's community of choice.

The CBR Centre in Solo is supported by the International Centre for the Advancement of Community Based Rehabilitation (ICACBR) at Queen's University in Ontario, Canada. ICACBR is a Centre of Excellence for CBR funded by the Canadian government. The Council of Canadians with Disabilities (CCD) is one of ICACBR's partnership organizations. Disability research and advocacy is advanced through ICACBR, and CBR projects like those in Solo benefit from this expertise and support.

THE EMERGENCE OF CBR

CBR as an effective disability strategy was officially recognized by the World Health Organization (WHO) in 1978, in response to the huge challenges facing people with disabilities in developing countries.[2] CBR was intended to reach as large a number of people as possible in the most cost-effective and culturally appropriate way.[3] CBR projects are developed through partnerships between rehabilitation professionals, persons with disability, their families and the broader community. Partnership provides a way to transfer skills and knowledge to the grassroots of communities. Self-help skills are meant to empower disabled people to take control of the decisions that affect their lives.

One of the major tasks of CBR is training both CBR volunteers and the broader community. Reaching women in these communities is a key focus of the Solo CBR Centre.

WOMEN AND THE SOLO CBR PROJECT

The CBR philosophy and the Solo CBR Centre value the participation of women, especially disabled women. This is for two reasons: first, reaching families through women, mostly mothers, means disability messages find a larger audience; second, women have been missed by health and disability projects in the past, a neglect the Solo CBR Centre wants to change. However, CBR projects must remember that women and older female children are already the primary family caregivers. This burden is multiplied when the woman is also disabled.[4] CBR must take care not to overburden such women.

There is strong agreement in academic literature that women suffer the most as they struggle for daily survival.[5] Women in developing countries are responsible for both their own and their families' subsistence; they also provide water, prepare food and care for people who are sick. Women in developing countries experience the triple oppression of national underdevelopment, rural (and urban) poverty and patriarchy. Although the economies in Southeast Asia are developing faster than many others, in countries like Indonesia, women still face the hardships of poverty, disease, disability and lack of educational and employment opportunities.[6] Even access to basic health care is frequently lacking. WHO reports that, in 1993 alone, "more than 500,000 women died during pregnancy, and the number is rising ..."[7] Lack of knowledge about disability, combined with poor rehabilitation services and not enough commitment and financial resources means that many preventable disabilities often produce lifelong problems.[8] Here again, disabled women are likely to suffer additional disadvantage. They are more likely to live a life in complete isolation or abandonment, and are at much greater risk of abuse and violence.[9] The social forces that act in consort to oppress disabled women are clearly great.

THE SOLO CBR PROJECT AND ITS BENEFITS

Women who take part in CBR activities can expect several positive outcomes. First, CBR promotes positive attitudes about disability and uses technologies and strategies that fit the community and the culture. This also increases the status of women within the community. By emphasizing what disabled people (including women) can do rather than what they cannot, new talents and abilities are discovered. For example, as mentioned earlier, Parwati found a job that employed her love of fabrics and sewing. Similarly, Diah's exposure to CBR increased her self-confidence and helped her decide to work for the cause of disabled people as a CBR cadre.

A second benefit is that disabled women and women with disabled children have more opportunity to meet each other at the *posyandus*, where many CBR activities take place.[10] By gathering together and sharing experiences at monthly meetings, women can support each other in their efforts to care for their families. The CBR project in Solo, Indonesia, has added disability awareness and education to the list of *posyandu* activities. Therefore, during every monthly visit, women benefit from disability screening and, if a disability is identified in their child or themselves, additional support may be arranged. The Solo CBR Centre has developed simple disability booklets that can be given to families to help them care for a disabled family member. There are more than thirteen manuals in the series including: Helping to Prevent Disability; Helping a Person Move; Helping Children Who Have Difficulty Eating and Drinking; Helping Children With Mental Handicap and Those

With Behaviour Problems; Helping a Person Who Has Had a Stroke; and Finding Out About CBR.

The third benefit of the Solo project is that disabled people — particularly disabled women, who usually do not get as much formal schooling — have a chance to further their health education.[11] CBR training includes studying the causes of disability and removing the stigma attached to having a disability. Participants in CBR projects learn new ways to help disabled people through increased knowledge about how to prevent disabilities and how to help keep people living at the highest level of their physical and/or mental abilities. Finding ways to include the disabled person in normal community events is also important. For interested and motivated persons who have not had the opportunity to attend school, CBR training can offer a great deal of personal development. Occasionally, a person's increased knowledge and the skills they have learned as a volunteer lead to paid employment.

Fourth, disabled women who participate in CBR also benefit from increased contact with other disabled women. The positive impact of role models is a very important part of CBR's emphasis on community participation. When a disabled woman sees with her own eyes how another disabled woman is involved in community life, she wants to do the same. Positive role models are powerful agents of change. CBR helps find role models and supports networks of mutual self-help. The social activities that develop also strengthen communication and the emotional bonds between women in different communities. For CBR cadres, ongoing training courses often permit travel beyond one's local village to see how others have dealt with disability issues. Larger networks of support mean that disabled women have more choice and more ways to become equal participants in their home communities.

Fifth, CCD involvement on behalf of ICACBR has strengthened the disability movement in Indonesia. Francine Arsenault, past president of CCD, recalls numerous occasions when, just by their presence at meetings of medical professionals and government health officials, disabled women showed that they have abilities and important concerns to share. During one visit to Solo to conduct CBR training, Francine shared a hotel room with a partially sighted woman from Jakarta. Francine recalls staying up late into the night describing how she talks with politicians in Canada and how she first began organizing people with disabilities to fight for their rights. She is convinced that written resource materials are essential for the development of new disability organizations. However, she believes her personal story and real-life experience is a powerful motivator too, in particular for disabled women who may not have seen this level of confidence and success before. Her impact as a role model has been great. In another meeting with villagers, Francine remembers asking how many of the 19 disabled people in the village were married. There was complete silence. The community had only thought of disabled people as needing homes, food, clothes etc. They had not thought about their social needs. Francine used this opportunity to talk about her husband and her children. It was a powerful opportunity to shape attitudes and expectations — a very important part of her work.[12]

Finally, disabled women's participation in the Solo CBR project means increased personal prestige and status.[13] The Solo project has received a lot of international attention over the last decade. Its commitment to the principles of overall community development and its emphasis on the key role played by disabled people themselves has contributed greatly to its positive reputation. In the end, whether the success of the Solo project can be explained by the underlying traditional value of *gotong-royung* (mutual self-help) or whether it is due to individual self-determination and empowerment, the actual outcome for women with disabilities is the same. And disabled people, including women, will continue to reap the rewards.

ONGOING CHALLENGES FOR CBR

Although persons with disabilities have received a lot of benefits from CBR projects like the one in Solo, Indonesia, the international movement for community based disability projects is looking at several issues. These challenges include, but are not limited to, the nature of culture and communities, power and social control. These international challenges affect how CBR works in Indonesia.

First, Indonesia is a Muslim country, where women are traditionally not community decision-makers. How do disability projects respect local religious and cultural structures and practices while improving the status, power and control of women? In other words, how do projects ensure that women's voices are heard?[14] Likewise, how can we make sure that the talk about "community participation" and "empowerment" does not become talk about women's "care," leaving women less, not more, empowered in the end?[15]

The second challenge facing CBR is avoiding the still too common "top-down" quality of disability projects. The way in which disability workers are chosen is one example of this. In many disability projects, CBR workers are selected by village headmen, who favour women who already have high prestige and power within the community. This is strategic; cadre participation will be sustained by enhancing personal position within the community, and this will help to ensure that the village complies with project objectives. But it is not clear who makes the best cadre. Careful analysis of the mix of CBR workers must be made and the question of who can legitimately speak for the community must be asked. For example, males, females and disabled cadres alike must be looked at for class and ethnic biases.[16] It is likely that all CBR workers hope to get, as well as give, in their position, so the possibility that they may spend too much time looking out for their own interests must always be carefully considered.

The third challenge — one which is sometimes surprising to people who support community-based disability projects in the West — is that disabled people do not always choose community participation and empowerment as the way to improve their quality of lives. Rather, they may demand institutional, professional and highly technical services, insisting that governments, not individuals, are responsible for this task. Disabled people in all parts of the world want choice. Choices must not only be available but also respected. If disabled people refuse to support disability projects without having reached prior agreement about the project and the amount of money or staff the government will provide, we should not be taken off guard.[17] CBR will have to grow to make room for different categories of disabled persons and will have to be open towards referring persons to supportive medical treatment and other more specialized services.[18] Just as CBR must not become a second-class rehabilitation service, the future demands more flexibility and responsiveness from CBR than ever before.

CONCLUSION

It has been suggested by the Asia Partnership for Human Development (APHD) that the way to move ahead in international community disability work is to listen more carefully to the voices of women.[19] The disability researchers French and Petersen say that, while women's perspectives are essential, we should look carefully at the forces in society that systematically remove women, especially disabled women, from positions of power.[20] These researchers stress that uncritical support of empowerment carries with it significant risks: If individual empowerment is the main focus of community-based disability initiatives, then important structural factors, such as how economic systems, labour and health services are organized, will not get the public attention they require. Emphasis on individual empowerment also risks hiding diversity — and sometimes even tensions and conflicts — within groups of women. Finally, researchers Cottone and Cottone caution against empowering women if empowerment means they are expected to help themselves with little help from society.[21]

The Roeher Institute has recently looked at the social support for disabled persons in Canada.[22] They have said that, while security, democracy and citizenship have formed a necessary foundation for longterm social well-being, the foundation is inadequate. Their report, *Social Well-being: A Paradigm for Reform*, calls for the addition of two further key concepts to the social foundation — self-determination and equality. These concepts were quickly recognized as founding principles of the disability rights movement. The Roeher Institute policy document stresses that self-reliance simply cannot address the social inequalities that still exist between persons with disabilities and those without disabilities. Finding the political will to change these inequalities is absolutely necessary or the gap between "the haves and the have-nots" will grow.

The impact of organizations of disabled people must not be ignored. For example, Francine Arsenault of CCD has seen major changes within the Solo CBR project over the years of her involvement. In the beginning, professionals trained local volunteers to identify disabled people and to provide them with simple, low-cost equipment. Today, in large part through the efforts of CCD and other disabled peoples' organizations in neighbouring countries, the Solo CBR project has expanded its focus to include the knowledge and experience of disabled persons themselves. By encouraging disabled persons to form organizations and meet each other, the disability movement in Indonesia has been strengthened. It can now advocate for legislative change and improved government services — the first steps toward a better life for all Indonesians with disabilities.

The political opportunity to include people with disabilities in community life has always existed, but disabled people feel much more needs to be done. Disabled women who have experienced the power of mutual self-help in their own lives are struggling to reach other women whose disadvantages remain significant. Researchers Racino and Heumann suggest that coalitions of disabled persons and other disadvantaged groups hold promise. By banding together in large groups, all those who are powerless may be heard.[23] With respect to community-based disability projects in particular, an experienced disability activist in Mexico says the most appropriate programmes are those that:

> ... *enable us; that help us to empower ourselves, so that we join with other disadvantaged and socially concerned groups, locally and globally, to work toward changing the power structures that deny us our basic rights to meet our needs and potentials.*[24]

For Diah and Parwati in Solo, Indonesia, personal courage, family support, mutual self-help, and specific disability services were all necessary to improve their quality of life. This may be called empowerment, but it is surely a complex process that still does not happen often enough.

NOTES

1. WHO, *Disability Prevention and Rehabilitation: Report of the WHO Expert Committee, Technical Report Series No. 668,* (Geneva: WHO, 1981), pp. 11-2.

2. WHO, 1981, pp. 12-3.

3. Chermak, G., "A global perspective on disability: A review of efforts to increase access and advance social integration for disabled persons," *International Disability Studies* 12, (1990), pp. 123-7; and ILO, UNESCO and WHO, "Community-based rehabilitation (CBR) for and with people with disabilities," Joint Position Paper, (Geneva: ILO, UNESCO and WHO, 1994), pp. 1-4.

4. Deegan, M., and N. Brooks, *Women and disability: The double handicap*, (New Brunswick, NJ, USA: Transaction Books, 1985), p. 1; and Symke, P., *Women and Health*, (London, England: Zed Books, 1991), pp. 1-8.

5. Boylan, E., *Women and Disability*, (London, England: Zed Books, 1991), pp. 1-22; and Grant, J., "One hundred and fifty million disabled children and growing," *One-in-Ten* 13 (1994), pp. 1-8.

6. Abernethy, V., "The world's women: Fighting a battle, losing the war," *Journal of Women's Health* 2, 1 (1993), pp. 7-16; Fuller, T., J. Edwards, S. Sermsri and S. Vorakitphokatorn, "Gender and health: Some Asian evidence," *Journal of Health and Social Behavior* 34 (1993), pp. 252-71; Koblinsky, M., J. Timyan and J. Gay, *The health of women: A global perspective*, (Boulder, CO, USA: Westview Press, 1993), pp. 1-195; and Lee, M., J. Hezekiah and D. Watters, "Rural women and power in Pakistan," *Health Care for Women International* 16 (1995), pp. 125-33.

7. Stackhouse, J., "Why health is a motherhood issue," *The Globe and Mail*, (Toronto, Canada: February 8, 1994), p. A13.

8. MacCormack, C., "Health and the social power of women," *Social Science and Medicine* 26 (1988), pp. 677-83.

9. Murthy, R.S., "Roles in CBR — family, volunteers, women," Unpublished paper presented at the Asia Regional Symposium on Research and Evaluation in CBR, (Bangalore, India: December 5-7, 1994), p. 2.

10. Lysack, C., "Community participation and community-based rehabilitation: An Indonesian case study," *Occupational Therapy International* 2, 3 (1995), pp. 149-65.

11. Lysack, C., and L. Krefting, "Community based rehabilitation cadres and their motivation for volunteerism," *International Journal of Rehabilitation Research* 16 (1993), pp. 133-41.

12. Arsenault, F., personal communication (January 17, 1996).

13. Lysack and Krefting, 1993.

14. Parpart, J., "Who is the 'other'?: A postmodern feminist critique of women and development theory and practice," *Development and Change* 24 (1993), pp. 439-64.

15. Stehlik, D., "Untying the knot: A socialist-feminist analysis of the social construction of care," *Social Research and Development*, Monograph No. 7, (Perth, Australia: Centre for the Development of Human Resources, Edith Cowan University, 1993), pp. 14-53; and Lysack, C., and L. Krefting, "The myths of volunteerism and the women who make community based rehabilitation work," *CBR News* 17 (London, England: May-August, 1994), p. 5.

16. Cottone, L., and R. Cottone, "Women and disabilities: On the paradox of empowerment and the need for a trans-systemic and feminist perspective," *Journal of Applied Rehabilitation Counselling* 23, 4 (1992), pp. 20-5; and Morris, J., "Feminism and disability," *Feminist Review* 43 (Spring, 1993), pp. 57-70.

17. Cocks, E., "Encouraging a paradigm shift in services for people with disabilities," *Social Research and Development*, Monograph No. 9, (Perth, Australia: Centre for the Development of Human Resources, Edith Cowan University, 1994), pp. 1-57.

18. Vanneste, G., "Singing in the rain: Demystifying community-based rehabilitation," unpublished paper, (Christoffel Blindenmission International, Butare, Rwanda: 1994), p. 8.

19. Asia Partnership for Human Development, *Awake: Asian women and the struggle for justice*, (Sydney, Australia: Asia Partnership for Human Development, 1985), pp. 7-11.

20. French, S., "Researching disability: The way forward," *Disability and Rehabilitation* 14, 4 (1992), pp. 183-6; and Petersen, A., "Community development in health promotion: Empowerment or regulation?" *Australian Journal of Public Health* 18, 2 (1994), pp. 213-17.

21. Cottone, L., and R. Cottone, 1992.

22. The Roeher Institute, *Social Well Being: A Paradigm for Reform*, (Toronto, Canada: The Roeher Institute, 1993), pp. 27-42.

23. Racino, J., and J. Heumann, "Independent living and community life," *Aging and disabilities* 16, 1 (1992), pp. 43-7.

24. Werner, D., "Strengthening the role of disabled people in community based rehabilitation programs," unpublished paper presented at a workshop on community-based rehabilitation, (Solo, Indonesia: November 22-26, 1994), p. 2.

Mary Mitchell, *Jamaica*

Hard Luck

Loss of sight is a plight.
So hard luck, no work.
Lord it's a dread.
What a life!
Times hard!

We walk on the street
Every person we meet
Lord dear, she blind.
What a time — poor thing.
What a sin.

We have our dignity.
Don't treat us with impunity.
All we really need is the opportunity!

So what!
We are capable.
Stop your lie.
Hear our cry.
Give us a try.

You will find that
We are well able
Yes, we are well able.

So, who is to blame,
If we have no claim to fame.
All are human beings — just the same.

So hard luck, no work.
Lord it's a dread.
What a life!
Times hard!

Michele Green, *Canada*

Love Conquers All?

I never thought much about babies,
for years — only my career.
In graduate school, I got used to hearing
some professors mumble just loud enough
that blind people couldn't be historians.
I learned what to ignore and when to fight back.
Still, it took me so long and it was such hard work
that there was only room and love enough
in my life for me and my husband.
Mostly life was just about me.

This year, however, curled up in the weak Christmas sunshine,
I cannot ignore the ticking of my biological clock.
I want to have a baby.
That is, I'm pretty sure that I want to have a baby.
Reason does not rule here.
I used to think
blind women ought not to have babies; it's not fair to either.
But that constant ticking warns me:
choose soon or forever hold my peace.

Sometimes my best friend lets me babysit
Cuddling this eight month wonder,
smelling his baby smell,
touching his fuzzy hair,
listening to his cooing and gurgling,
I yearn for my own baby.
But I'm uneasy, nervous
that this most precious being may come to harm
as he crawls out of my narrow range of sight.
Both my friend and I really know
my "favour" of babysitting
is the ultimate test of her trust.

More disturbing, is my husband's uncertainty,
unspoken —
he's always supported me in every decision —
but loud enough for me to hear.
A child?

And, really,
who am I to decide to pass on
my unpredictably defective gene?
Heads — my baby's blind; tails — she's sighted.
And how will I feed my baby, keep her clean?
How will I keep her safe —
from the stairs, the stove, the street?
Everything is a potential peril.

I ache knowing that I won't see
the first smile, the first step,
the first time she reaches out to me.
I tremble to think she might not take that first step,
or reach out,
because she can't see others doing what seems so natural.

Will she grow up secure and confident
if I can't see her finger painting pictures,
or her acting debut in the school play,
or help her pick out her prom dress?
Will she feel obligated to become the parent, guiding, helping me?
Could I have a child and then rob her of her childhood?

Watching myself slowly go blind
has been eased by having the time to accommodate,
to achieve, to collect and store precious visual memories.
My child might not have that time.
And knowing that her struggle may be harder than mine,
that this world has little time or care
for the less than perfect,
I will wait in dread for the day she asks,
"Why did you have me?"

There is a fighting voice inside me,
sometimes strong enough to silence the fears,
that lists the ways to cope and adapt:
husband, grandparents, support groups, special pre-schools,
technological aids, orientation and mobility training.
Independent living skills. Advocacy for the disabled.

That voice proclaims that love can conquer all.
I recount other women with disabilities
who are nurturing, successful parents.
But I can't escape the picture of *my* baby
with a bell around her neck like a cat,
or on a leash like a dog.

Am I pessimistic or realistic?
selfish, or selfless?
lioness or mouse?
Do I need more courage? faith? restraint?
a sense of humour?
Which will win, the love and the longing, or the fear?

This year, curled up in the weak Christmas sunshine,
there are no answers.
But there is a cruel joke in my confusion.
Confessing my fears,
I must now question
my own intolerance of blindness,
of myself,
because this all feels too damn hard.

Francine Arsenault

A Global Flavour

At the second Disabled Peoples' International (DPI) Conference in 1985 in the Bahamas, Dr. Fatima Shah, a blind disability leader from Pakistan, demanded that women, who comprise 50 percent of the population, have at least equal representation on the board of directors of DPI. She and the majority of the female delegates threatened to form their own group and not to support the men of DPI. This was my first initiation into the diversity of views, cultures and traditions of differently-abled women from around the world!

For a country girl from an isolated, rural Ontario, Canada, setting who had been taught by her Scottish ancestors that a man was king in his home and that it was a woman's duty to support his every endeavour, this was a rude awakening. I had felt that my only role in this life was that of wife to Richard and mother to David, Kathleen and Jamie. I began to see that, although you need not stand on a street corner and shout how great you are, you should be able to assert your abilities, and should not hide your talents in order to make others appear superior.

Within a year of the conference, I had the opportunity to meet with women in the Caribbean. Eloise Rhone, a woman who, like me, had polio, spoke of her dream to be a teacher and the hard work she had put into planning to get the training she needed. She inspired me. Eloise's example, like that of so many other Caribbean Island women with disabilities, showed me that I was limiting myself. Perhaps, I thought, what people in the disability movement saw as my leadership skills needed to be further developed. Without letting my family down, I needed to stretch myself to learn about the issues. I needed to be able to speak out in a knowledgeable way. With my peers' support, I began to accomplish more than I had ever believed possible.

At about this time in my life, I was happily married but aware that my role as mother was drawing to a close — my youngest boy was 14, my daughter 20 and my eldest son 22. My health was showing evidence of postpolio slow down, so I decided it was time to become more involved in helping others and, in the process, help myself. Between 1981 and 1986, I became an advocate for people with disabilities at the local, regional, provincial, national and international levels.

At the first disability conference I attended, the delegates elected me chairperson for my region and a representative at the provincial level. The provincial organization, in turn, nominated me to the national organization and I had already been asked by a university group to do international work in Jamaica. In 1991, while representing the Council of Canadians with Disabilities (CCD), I sat on the board of directors of the International Centre for the Advancement of Community Based Rehabilitation (ICACBR) at Queen's University. The partners at ICACBR included universities and non-governmental organizations (NGOs) from Canada, India (Bombay and Allahabad), Indonesia and Bangladesh. Part of my role as a board member of ICACBR was to attend conferences in Dhaka and Jakarta, as a speaker, workshop leader and role model. I soon learned that, whether forums were in Australia, El Salvador, Grenada or Bombay, the issues for people with disabilities were the same.

The disabled women I met in Bangladesh at the ICACBR National Forum in 1992 were very resourceful, and yet very reticent about speaking out or coming forward with their suggestions. When I was asked to be a role model and give a keynote address at the forum, I overheard an argument between the conference coordinator and other guest speakers (mostly Muslim men) who refused to sit at the table with a disabled woman. I reminded them that I represented one of the co-sponsors of the event (ICACBR) and so had paid for their participation! No wonder women with disabilities lack confidence if they must battle such negative attitudes about their right to represent themselves.

At another seminar I attended in 1992, in Indonesia, Dr. Handjo Tjandrakusuma, an ICACBR partner who is considered the founder of CBR in Asia and runs the Yayasaan Pembinaan Anak Cacat (YPAC) Centre for Community Based Rehabilitation (CBR) in Indonesia, discussed how his centre had focused on prevention in their CBR project. They had established "Well Baby Clinics" that provide early detection of disabilities and medical rehabilitation. He conceded, however, that they had not yet been able to look at the social and economic situation of disabled adults returning to, or becoming a full part of, their communities. As if to confirm this problem, the workshops I facilitated in 1992 included only one or two disabled persons. By 1994, 54 disabled delegates took my course as part of their ongoing training as CBR cadres.

One of the wonderful benefits of taking part in the Indonesian seminar each year was that I always shared a room with another woman involved in the disability movement in her country. In 1993, my roommate was Ariani Mohammed from Jakarta, Indonesia, who is a member of Disabled Peoples' International (DPI). In 1994, I was matched up with Shushila Paudel from Katmandu, Nepal, who works with disabled women.

Ariani is a traditional Muslim wife. Her faithful commitment to her religion mirrored my own staunch Catholic upbringing. On numerous occasions, we spoke about the lack of women representatives on the DPI Indonesia board of directors and the difficulties Muslim women experience in going beyond the traditional role established for them within their homes. She and I both were in the enviable position of having husbands who support us financially and emotionally, thereby giving us the time and energy to work as volunteers. Other colleagues had to work every spare minute just to support themselves rather than being able to spend their time assisting others. Ariani was finally elected to the DPI board in 1993 and also began a woman's group for the visually impaired.

Shushila, on the other hand, had some support from her brother but really had to extend herself to do volunteer work in Nepal. Her beauty and regal appearance turn many heads but, still, she is often seen simply as a disabled woman. She is not given credit for her discerning mind and physical capabilities. From her, I learned how to find serenity, how to build self-confidence and about the importance of researching the people and events you will be discussing.

In the fall of 1994, I participated in an ICACBR symposium about research and education through CBR in Bangalore, India. N.S. Hema attended some of the workshops I facilitated. She astounded me with her common sense and simple wisdom. Not only were we soul-mates, we delighted each other with humorous family stories. We also shared our respect for our own culture and heritage and our faithful observance of religious beliefs. Hema invited me to share a meal with her in her home, and her hospitality was generous. When we toured the Association for the Physically Handicapped (APH) in Bangalore, some of Hema's organizational skills became very apparent. Hema uses her intuitive understanding of others, her lobbying, her facilitation of community cooperation and her fundraising skills to the best of her ability. Hema is more than an honorary president of her organization — she actively works to guide other disabled women to their highest potential, thereby benefiting their communities and the larger society.

I have been lucky to be able to meet so many inspirational women, and I am honoured to be a role model, showing others that, as a disabled woman, you can still have someone love you, have a family and be a full and active member of your community, if that is your wish. Inner strength and persistence in seeking goals can result in many successes. Persons with disabilities can become living examples of adaptability, consideration for others and solidarity for the common good.

Snapshot from Beijing
Interview by E. Catherine Boldt

Jamala Albaidhni
Yemen Society for Rehabilitation of the Physically Handicapped

In general, the situation of disabled women is extremely difficult. What makes it more difficult is that parents are not cooperative and they are not willing to let their disabled daughters go out of the house for treatment or for anything like that.

To bring disabled women to my organization for training or rehabilitation or education — the first step of getting them out of their houses — is the most difficult one. It is difficult to get them out of the house because of the situation of women in general in Yemen — although we are not daunted, actually. This is the last chunk of our work: to get over this first step. Just recently, parents are starting to understand the need of their disabled daughters to leave the house for services, training, education and for the process of integration.

At the least, the disabled woman should be equal to a disabled man. This is a starting point in terms of accessibility to services, and in terms of integration and participation in a number of fields in different levels. So, at least, she [the disabled woman] is equal to the disabled man — we are not talking about the able-bodied yet — this is a first starting point.

Shingirai Pensado, *Zimbabwe*

My Mother

My mother
You are special and exquisite
You are so many things to me
Only you in my eyes

People laugh at you
Talk, whisper and gossip
But you have turned a deaf ear
Relatives and friends no longer visit
But they don't see

They shout as you pass
Do I shit in the house?
Does someone feed me?
Does someone wash my clothes?
No! I do it all myself

In their eyes I'm a cabbage
Waiting to be watered
They can't accept me as I am
Though I've accepted disability

Mother, I don't mind
As long as you love me
But your heart rages inside
I can tell.

Shingirai Pensado, *Zimbabwe*

Why

My life is full of wishes
My heart never stops aching
Why such heartache when I have got a head?
My mind is like a traffic line full of vehicles

My mind is never at rest
Where will I get rest?
I am always thinking of today and tomorrow
My tears are my livelihood
For others it comes from sweat
Without shedding a tear

It's like I know no one in this world
For why should I suffer like this?
Because there is a difference
Between you and me
A difference I did not ask for
That is the reason for the difference

I recall
Yesterday it was taboo, we used to be locked
In houses like prisoners, until death crept on us
But today it's a different story, we can now sit
and gossip in the sunshine
But still I am not considered as an equal
But why should I be deprived of my rights
Am I not an individual like others?

I want my rights, so that I can have a share in my life
To speak out and to make decisions
The way you see and treat me, is hell on earth
You look down on me, like I am a wheelbarrow
Which needs pushing each day of its life
You are satisfied when you see me suffering
That's when you give the best of your smiles

I no longer feel comfortable when I am walking
Because your eyes never leave my body
You whisper and scratch each other
But why, I ask you?
Haven't you or don't you know the likes of me?
I am not the only one
When will this discrimination, degradation end.

Shingirai Pensado, *Zimbabwe*

The Me the World Doesn't See

I am like every woman you see
Fit and strong in mind
Always scratching my head like scraping a pot of porridge
To find new ideas and memories of the past

The world always shuns me
When I try to raise a point
It's like I'm cutting meat with a blunt knife
Everyone turns a deaf ear

My heart always pumps
The days of my life are telescoped into each other
I see black night everywhere
Life to me is the same old story
Full of pain and desire to be understood

I am beautiful as a nut
But who can see my beauty
When I'm covered by a shell?
Who will break the shell for me?

I am longing to see the sun
I've been mature for ages
I'm smooth as an olive
As bright as a glowing candle

I can't live a life of imagination
I don't need rescue
I have got my own ambition
I know my direction and my values.

Lizzie (Mamvura) Langshaw

Working Hard: The Nswazi Women's Group

The Nswazi Women's Group started in 1989, with help from the National Council of Disabled Persons of Zimbabwe (NCDPZ) Women's Group Development Programme. As a group, we are fully aware of the rights of women with disabilities. The NCDPZ Nswazi Women's Group is very lucky because the community encourages us to work hard and have more ventures in Nswazi area.

Nswazi women were mobilized into a pressure group by the Women's Group Development Programme. We have an executive that is composed of ten women and is chaired by Betty Mzira and our membership is close to 350 women, including women with disabilities, mothers of disabled children and women married to disabled men. The Nswazi group is doing so well in the field of advocacy and referrals that the Women's Group Development Programme is quite pleased: Nswazi can be used as a role model for other projects.

At the end of 1990, the Nswazi Women's Group came up with a number of ideas for projects. We finally agreed to start a grinding mill to give jobs and money to women

and children with disabilities in our community. The group gener-
ated even more interest when, around this time, we received 380
dollars from Alma Associates Filming Company (based in the UK)
for taking part in the production of an NCDPZ documentary. We
used the money to run seminars and workshops at group level on
how to use a grinding mill. Thanks to the workshops, the group is
full of rich information on advocacy and on running a business.

The Nswazi Women's Group also used part of the money to
carry out a survey. We asked people in the Nswazi community if
they needed a grinding mill and whether they would grind their
maize at a mill owned by women with disabilities. The results of
this survey were discussed at a meeting of the Women's Group
Development Programme personnel, the headmen and the members themselves.

The results showed that people (women, of course) had to travel
tens of kilometres to the nearest grinding mill; hence, a grinding
mill at Mabechu Growth Point in Nswazi was a good idea. The
question of women with disabilities owning the mill was immate-
rial. The headman blessed the group by offering his support. The
community offered to help women with disabilities in all their
endeavours. As an organization, the Women's Group Development
Programme was left without any doubt that the Nswazi Women's
Group was able to run and monitor a business.

The authorities at the Rural District Council had really negative
attitudes towards Nswazi women because they wanted to come up
with a grinding mill plan themselves. As a result, they took their
time to approve the plan. Members of NCDPZ and the Nswazi
Women's Group went there in person or phoned them. We were
always told to change something in the plan. After months of waiting,
the plan was finally approved. At this point, the Council's Financial
Controller, D. Zulu, requested funds from the Council of Canadians
with Disabilities (CCD) on behalf of the Nswazi Women's Group.
With the money from CCD, the much-cherished mill was bought for
the group.

When the mill was completed, we invited the District Rural
Council to come and inspect the mill house. They were impressed,
in spite of giving us a hard time. What is most ironic is that, now,
they talk so well about the work of women with disabilities. They
say that our mill house is the best in the area. Men in the Nswazi

community, including the headmen of various communities around here, are very supportive of us. If there is anything hard to be done at the mill house, the men are quick to assist. Actually, the men are always at the mill house, playing cards or selling vegetables to women who come to grind their maize and men such as the caretaker and the person who banks our money every Wednesday assist at the mill. They are quite happy to report about the daily activities to the women on duty. Having the mill in Nswazi has made the men appreciate the existence of disabled women more.

People in Nswazi have a lot to say about the mill and how it has changed the lives of women with disabilities. The women with disabilities who work at the mill have employment and are role models in the community. The stories below show how members are directly benefiting from proceeds of the mill, although there are many more women who had some help from the Nswazi Women's Group for individual projects like sewing, knitting, poultry and goat-keeping.

Buhle Ndlovu is a mother of three boys. Two are in high school. She was divorced by her husband because of her disability. She works so hard to see her children through school. The Nswazi Women's Group referred her to the Department of Social Welfare for assistance, who then started to pay the school fees for Buhle's boys.

To help Buhle become financially sound, she was given some money from the proceeds of the mill to start her individual project. Buhle is into poultry, so she was sent by the group for training in chicken rearing. In Zimbabwe, a visitor must be given sadza and chicken within a day of their arrival. This is to show that the host appreciates the visit. Because of this cultural norm, and because families like to eat chicken, people keep chickens at home. Buhle alleviates the problem for those who do not have their own chickens. She sells her chickens for 26 to 30 dollars, depending on the person who is buying the chicken. Buhle also sometimes exchanges her chickens for maize or clothes and resells the maize and clothes to the community. This keeps her busy all the time. Her children's father would like to take her back because she is an industrious woman. But Buhle is not prepared to do that because she is very independent.

Buhle says the money she gets from the sales of maize, clothes and chickens buys food and clothes, and pays part of the school fees for her children — her project is viable. One day, Buhle hopes to open a kiosk at her home where she will sell groceries and other things.

Bongi Mukhahla is very small in spite of his age. He can't talk, walk or sit. He lives with his grandparents and, most of the time, he is in the kitchen sleeping. He stays in the kitchen because his grandmother spends most of her time in the kitchen, cooking or keeping an eye on Bongi. Bongi's father would not marry his mother because of Bongi. His mother has since remarried, but the stepfather is not interested in Bongi. Hence, Bongi remains with his grandparents.

Bongi needs special food that neither his grandparents nor his mother are able to provide for him. The Nswazi Women's Group proposed that children like Bongi should be assisted as much as possible. Fifty chicks plus food were bought for Bongi by the Nswazi women. The grandmother sees to the smooth running of Bongi's project. She was sent for training on how to budget — how to bank Bongi's money from the sale of the chickens and buy the required food for Bongi. This project goes on throughout the year. Bongi is fed and clothed like any other child — maybe even better.

As you can see from these stories, the lives of our women members have changed for the better. They are independent financially. Their children with disabilities are protected. The Nswazi Women's Group makes sure that money for the children is looked after well and the community respects women with disabilities.

Some men and women in the community have approached the Nswazi Women's Group. They think the group should venture into opening a store because we are so capable. The men in the area — including disabled men — appreciate the capabilities of the Nswazi women. Aided by proceeds from the grinding mill, the group is putting money into more individual projects. Men are keen to join in the projects. However, the women who need assistance are many and the group wants to uplift the status of women first. In spite of this, men continue to support us morally.

Our sincere gratitude goes to CCD for supporting the Nswazi women. Next time you are in Zimbabwe, please let us take you to Nswazi. We are into advocacy and individual projects for economic empowerment. When there is food at home, all women are working hard — and so are Nswazi women.

Lizzie (Mamvura) Langshaw, *Zimbabwe*

My Feelings as a Disabled Woman

I'm growing up
And people think I will never go away
That I will always live with you
Be washed and fed by you — even at the age of twenty
The perfect offspring who never leaves the nest.

You teach me to be independent
A strong individual
To have my own opinions
To earn my own living
Neither of us knows
If one day — only one day — I will wash and dress myself
And live independently.

But I haven't been programmed to be anybody's wife
Lover
Or mother
You didn't teach me to serve anybody
To wash or peel potatoes.

People appreciate my intelligence
My wit and sharpness
Creativity and humour
You call me "*Mai reCock*"
Refusing to inoculate me against rubella.

You ignore my sexuality.

Justine Kiwanuka
Interview by Diane Driedger

Refugees with Disabilities: Living a Full Life in Canada

I left Uganda for Kenya in 1983. I was injured before I left Uganda. Because of my health conditions, I went straight into a hospital, not to a refugee camp. I was still undergoing treatment for the sustained injuries. All the time I was in Kenya, I wanted to go back home to Uganda. But after four years of being in Nairobi, I realized things were not getting any better in Uganda and there was no indication that I would be able to go back home soon. I realized I was just in transit. I figured out that I had to start leading a full life, and I had to start somewhere.

Through a contact I met in hospital, I applied to come to Canada. But, because of my disability, I was told I could not come unless I got a sponsorship. In this connection, I was lucky: The officer I was dealing with in the Canadian High Commission took it upon herself to look for sponsors — but usually it does not happen like that. Because of my disability, I would not have been able to come if I had not been sponsored. That is what I was told.

I have been living in Canada for seven years now. I went back to school and did volunteer work before and during school. I volunteered with the Independent Living Resource Centre in Winnipeg, with the Immigrant Access Service and within my church. When I came to Canada, I had some problems of adaptation, not unlike other immigrants. Nevertheless, I soon found my way around and was able to engage in worthwhile activities. My health problems were not any more serious than those of many Canadians I have seen. I do things non-disabled people can do, with limitations of course. If disabled people are not labelled as unable or invalid, they can lead a normal life and do things they want to do, within their abilities.

Often refugees with disabilities are very vulnerable in their first country of asylum, especially where there is not much infrastructure to cater to disabled refugees — these people are not a priority. Another problem is that it is not easy to get sponsorship for disabled people. Many are in refugee camps and they may not be allowed to leave the camps. Consequently, they are unable to make the necessary contacts which may lead to sponsorship. As a case in point, without sponsorship, disabled refugees are unable to achieve their dream of entering Canada or other countries.

Refugees are judged or classified by the United Nations High Commission for Refugees (UNHCR) as bonafide refugees only if the UNHCR declares them a genuine refugee with a well-grounded fear of persecution if they return to their home country. In addition, before refugees can come to Canada, they must be considered adaptable to Canadian society. However, refugees with disabilities may not pass the adaptability criteria for many reasons, including stereotyping on the basis of disability. In this case, disabled refugees can only get into Canada through direct sponsorship. I am a member of the Refugee Concerns Committee in my presbytery in Manitoba. We deal with refugees who do not fit the conventional refugee criteria, but who are in urgent need of protection and who can come under a designated class. Some are single women with children (classified as women at risk), disabled people and, sometimes, youths. They cannot come to Canada without sponsorship.

In the Refugee Concerns Committee, we have seen people with disabilities and families with disabled members who have applied to come to Canada but have been rejected on the basis of disability. For example, on one occasion a family was approved to come, but, after the immigration officials found out that one family member had a disability, the family was rejected.

There appear to be loopholes in the Canadian immigration system as far as disabled peoples' issues are concerned. For example, there seems to be no proactive policy in place which specifically caters to people with disabilities. Yet most disabled people cannot qualify under the adaptability criteria as it exists today. It would appear that the Canadian immigration system looks at disability mainly as a health issue and assumes that disabled people will cost the government more and will become welfare recipients. I am not implying that some people with disabilities do not have health needs, but simply stressing that not all disabilities are health problems. Also, disability issues as whole should not be labelled as health issues. This has traditionally been a way of eliminating and negating disabled people, and making them feel as though they are a burden to themselves as well as to society. Because of this traditional way of labelling disabled people, they are unable to come to Canada very easily or without sponsorship.

As Canadian immigration policy changes, so does the sponsorship. A few years ago, the government could jointly sponsor with churches or organizations; today, the government is asking the churches to take full responsibility for those people who fall under the categories of women at risk or people at risk. As a result, churches are trying to get together to co-sponsor refugees, when, previously, one church would take on a family by itself. Since there were not many sponsoring churches or organizations in the first place, you cannot help but wonder what is going to happen to such people and whether the churches will really be able to take on full responsibility for them.

Unfortunately, some of the recent changes further oppress the already oppressed recipients — such as disabled refugees. This is sad. The situation has been made worse by the imposition of a 975 dollar landing fee. This additional expense does not only impinge on refugees, who can barely find their daily bread, but also complicates sponsorship. For example, in a case where sponsors would like to bring in a family of four, it becomes very expensive since this landing fee is applied to each member of the family. The sponsors still have to worry about airfare, and the upkeep of the family once they arrive in Canada.

In my opinion, imposing a landing fee is another way of discriminating against, and leaving out, people in need, especially those from impoverished developing countries. The government is justifying the imposition of the landing fee by asserting that it is trying to reduce its debt. This justification ignores the fact that the people who come to this country do contribute to the growth of the economy, just like other Canadians. In fact, in the long term, immigration is profitable to the country.

As Canadians, we have earned our international status. Canada has built a reputation abroad as a country that opens its doors and that has been in the forefront of the struggle to end violations of human rights. It is unfortunate to see that Canada is one of the first countries to start imposing costly restrictions on refugees. The message that Canada is sending out is: "We have built our status both at home and internationally, so we do not need you now, except if you are bringing in money. When the time comes and we need you for our benefit, we shall open the doors again." This message from a country as wealthy as Canada is hard to defend.

As for disabled persons, they should be treated like other refugees. It is important for disability organizations to build links with local and national sponsoring churches and organizations and to work on increasing the number of disabled refugees who can find a new home. It is also necessary to change the ways that immigration policies deal with disabled refugees. There are very few people with disabilities who find sponsors to come to Canada or other countries. Yet the number of disabled refugees is enormous, and many are waiting in refugee camps in despair.

Snapshot from Beijing
Interview by E. Catherine Boldt

Theresa Mofomobe
Lesotho Union of Women with Disabilities

Theresa: I believe that all people are equal. However, there are some people who are denied equality. I believe in struggling every day until we get equality.

First of all, I think I'm talking from an African point of view. I have a feeling that women with disabilities in Africa need to be empowered and need to be trained in order to become leaders, in order to become stronger, in order to be in a position to articulate their needs. Currently, there are a few women with disabilities who are able to articulate their needs and problems, who are able to fight for their equality — but it is not yet a satisfactory number. Therefore, there is a need to empower women at all levels.

As women with disabilities from Africa, we really need to learn more from our sisters overseas, such as those in Canada. I am aware that women with disabilities in different organizations are quite active and have good experiences. So we really need to establish some information networking between Africa and our sisters in other countries.

Catherine: I would say, also, that we need to learn from you. If we continue to make an exchange, it would be best for all of us, because we all have a lot to learn. My philosophy is that we women with disabilities from every country, from every colour, from every ethnic background — we all are peers.

Theresa: That's right!

Catherine: We are all discriminated against in the same way, and I think that we have an advantage as a group because we are connected that way. We have to work together because we have so much in common.

Theresa: I agree with you. Beautiful!

E. Catherine Boldt

We Want Access *Now!*

I want to make it clear that I did not go to the non-governmental organizations' (NGOs) portion of the Fourth World Conference on Women in Beijing, China, solely as a representative of the disabilities movement. I went to China because I was selected as a result of my involvement in the Canadian women's movement — namely, as a representative of the Canadian Research Institute for the Advancement of Women (CRIAW). I am a member of the national board of CRIAW, and have had a long commitment to the women's movement which parallels my commitment to the disabilities community. CRIAW is committed to the concept of diversity, and has, in the past and present, had other women with disabilities serve on its board.

CRIAW was so supportive of my work as a woman with a disability that, when ordering business cards to pass out at the forum, they put the address of the Council of Canadians with Disabilities (CCD) on the usually blank side of the card. CRIAW was also wise enough to have both their name and mine translated into Mandarin. This proved to be very helpful and showed a certain respect for the country that was to be hosting us, as well as respect for all my areas of activism.

In preparation for the conference, the Canadian Beijing Facilitating Committee put out a call for nominated representatives of various organizations to go through a process of selection. They made it clear that diversity would be one of the priorities for the 40 delegates that they would choose. Out of 40 delegates, five women with disabilities were chosen (there may have been others, but they did not identify themselves to me). This approximates the ratio of Canadians with disabilities to the general Canadian population (about 10 to 14 percent of us identify ourselves as having a disability). Within this small faction of disabled women, we also represented quite a diverse range of disabilities. Only a wise woman wheelchair-user chose not to go after all — the reasons I call her wise will be evident after you read this article.

One of the most impressive aspects of the Beijing conference was the number of delegations, from so many countries, that included women with disabilities. There were women with disabilities from everywhere: China, South Korea, South Africa, Finland, Lebanon, the Ukraine, Mexico, Tirana, Albania, Ireland, Yemen, New Zealand, Kazakhstan, Bangladesh, Sri Lanka, Kenya, Nicaragua, Lesotho, Pakistan, Nepal, El Salvador, Tanzania, Thailand, Guatemala, Uganda, Sweden, Ethiopia, Russia, Australia, Peru, Mauritius, England, Malaysia and the United States. Japan even had a very large and well-organized delegation that included their own set of interpreters. And these were just the delegations that I encountered — there were probably more that I did not have the chance to meet.

All of these countries (and many more) gave women with disabilities the opportunity to take the initiative and have their voices heard at this historic event. Some of these women came as part of their countries' official delegations, some came in non-governmental organizations' (NGOs) delegations, others were fortunate enough to have been included in both. There were many women with disabilities sponsored by NGOs active in their own countries. Many women, like myself, did not come representing an organization of people with disabilities. Other women with disabilities had such a strong desire to be included, they came as individuals after expending great efforts to raise funds for themselves and, in some cases, an attendant. It took a great deal of determination for each and every delegate with a disability just to get through the front gate of the conference site.

Theresa Mofomobe from Lesotho Union of Women with Disabilities described her motivation to be included by her country:

> *At home, we established the so-called Lesotho Council of NGOs and Voluntary Organizations. In that council, they had a women's committee that was dealing with Beijing preparations. I realized that the women in that council did not realize the need to include the needs of women with disabilities. As a result, we requested that we sit on the committee in order to include the issues of women with disabilities at a national level. We also realized that they were still not sensitized to all our problems and I felt a need for us to be represented here [in Beijing] to share whatever will be discussed back home with our women with disabilities ... The congress that took place in 1985 in Kenya, which issued the Nairobi Forward Looking Strategies, did not include the issues of women with disabilities. CEDAW [the Convention on the Elimination of all Forms of Discrimination Against Women], which is already ratified in many countries, is very quiet about the issues of women with disabilities. Therefore, we had fear that the same thing would happen again here — that our issues would not be dealt with. We are here to have input into each and every workshop and, wherever possible, to talk about our issues.*

I am very glad that Theresa Mofomobe qualified her goal by saying she would want us to have input "wherever possible," as it became very difficult for most of us to get into the workshops and participate on an equal level. This was due to the lack of access on the site, difficulty with transportation and communication, and a lack of reliable volunteers.

It has been widely reported that the site of the conference had to be changed abruptly from Beijing to Huairou, which is 60 kilometres away. The reason given was that one of the buildings in Beijing was "structurally unsound" and unsafe for our purposes. The new site was very large and it was obviously made up very quickly, albeit with the best intentions. The paths were paved with uncured concrete pavers that crumbled and became loose in the heavy rain, as well as being crushed by the various vehicles that passed over them. This made the already uneven and treacherous terrain more difficult for women with disabilities. There were only one or two wheelchair ramps, and when it rained, the mud and sand made it impossible to manoeuvre safely.

Many of the women with wheelchairs bravely took the great chance of having untrained strangers carry them up stairs into buildings, many times up to the second or third floors. Sometimes, the carriers were men from the military with guns strapped to their hips. Proper vehicles for wheelchair transport were also unavailable. Buses with seats removed and long makeshift ramps were used to transport women wheelchair-users back and forth to their hotels. There was also no way to strap the wheelchairs down safely, thus making this ride — which took place twice daily and was an hour-and-a-half long — very treacherous.

The uneven surfaces, the many stairs, and the lack of elevators and ramps made being autonomous in a wheelchair an impossibility. Those of us with canes and crutches also could not manage the terrain, nor the distances between the site's many events. Neither was there any kind of shuttle vehicle available to go from one place to the next — something which could have also benefited older women participants. To make matters worse, the tent designated as the disabilities tent was situated in the farthest possible location at the site. It had very uneven surfaces and little ditches that had to be manoeuvred around. The stated reason for the distance to our tent was that our numbers were underestimated. The NGO forum office facility coordinator said they had expected about 140 women with disabilities. Originally, our tent was to be part of the diversity area, as disability fit into that theme — they saw us as matching that particular space very well. Yet over 200 women with disabilities had attended a pre-conference symposium held by Women's International Linkage on Disability, on August 29, 1995 in a rural hotel in China. As well, the Chinese Organizing Committee must not have relied on its own conference registration forms. Each and every delegate's registration form, whether they were disabled or not, surveyed physical needs. These needs included wheelchair-accessible transportation and bathroom access, as well as other appropriate accommodations. Because of the detailed questionnaire, we had thought that ways to take care of our needs would be put in place, but the site in no way accommodated the 400 to 500 (by my informal count) delegates with disabilities.

It took a great deal of effort for disabled delegates to make it to our tent; and, after reaching that destination, many of us had no reserves of energy left for walking about and searching for relevant and accessible workshops. Over and over again, we made the effort to search out a workshop, only to find that it had been moved to a different building, or that it was being held on the fifth floor of a building with no elevator, or that it had simply been cancelled.

In a *Toronto Star* article of September 2, 1995, Paul Watson of the Asian Bureau offered further testimony regarding the inaccessibility of the forum site. He reported back to Canada that, "The new site is a labyrinth of tents, schools, theatres, even a shooting range, linked by crumbling concrete patio tiles, dirt paths and staircases. It's a good hike for someone with strong legs, but a frustrating and sometimes impossible journey for delegates who can only get around in wheelchairs, on crutches or for those who can't see ... There is just one shuttle bus with a wheelchair ramp, which disabled delegates organized for themselves, and it runs on such a restricted schedule that it's almost useless ... Hundreds of outdoor toilets, the kind found at construction sites, are impossible for people in wheelchairs to use ... Disabled women have a lot to add in debates about any issues concerning women and they're silenced because they can't join the sessions."

The logistics of the site were not the only barriers; women who were blind were not provided with any materials in alternative media. The programme was not available in any other format besides print, which meant that women who were blind could only go to the events that they had been told about. Access to information on the site was already difficult, at best. This left the women with vision disabilities in a double bind. Volunteers were provided for assistance, but they had been given little or no training and many of them had never seen a disabled person before, let alone guided a blind person or pushed a wheelchair. Volunteers are not suitable for all personal tasks and were not available in the middle of the night when a crucial personal situation might require attention. Some volunteers ended up making warm friendships with those to whom they lent a hand, but many were not given enough training or information to be of much use.

The United Nations (UN) did not provide subsidies for interpreters for women who were deaf. Sign language does not have a universal lexicon and signing not only varies between countries, it also can differ within regions. There were no subsidies for women who needed attendants to help them with daily care. There were also no subsidies for women who were blind and had to travel very long distances in very confusing circumstances. Ironically, although there were no subsidies provided for anyone who needed assistance, many major airlines have policies that do not let a passenger identifying as a person with a disability fly unattended. Women who were experienced solo world travellers sometimes had to provide at least the appearance of a travelling companion just to get on a plane.

• • •

After spending a couple of days doing battle with the site and trying to get into various sessions and workshops, I decided that perhaps I would try to stick to workshops on the topic of disability, as surely they would be easy for me to access. Other women with disabilities must have had the same idea; each disability-themed workshop during the day had progressively more of us in attendance. The first workshop I went to was up on the second floor of a building that had no elevator. The presenter had difficulty getting up the stairs to present her paper. The second workshop with disability in the title turned out to be the same — it was on the second floor of a building with no elevator.

As the day progressed, you could feel the increased frustration of many of the women with mobility disabilities and the wheelchair-users. Unbelievably, the day's third workshop with disability in the title turned out to be even worse. It was in the Great Hall, a very imposing building in which the plenaries were held, where one flight of stairs was the equivalent of perhaps three in a regular building. This situation put all the women with disabilities — those who couldn't make it up the stairs as well as those who could — in a very difficult position, and pitted members of our own disabilities community against each other.

The presenters of this third workshop were women with disabilities, and they wanted a venue to present their very valuable work. Some of the women with disabilities could make it up the stairs and some of the women wheelchair-users were willing to be carried up that great distance. Others had had enough of being carried for one day, or, for various reasons, had decided it was not practical. This situation also affected a woman who was deaf, because her interpreter used a power scooter and could not be carried. We requested that the presenters try running their session in the lobby of the Great Hall or outside in front, in plain sight, so that people could see our struggles in these circumstances. But this certainly did not afford the presenters peace and quiet or the respect they deserved. We tried reasoning with the building manager to help us exchange our room for one on the first floor, but she claimed not to have the power to arrange such details. Besides, the other sessions were well underway by this time.

Our group soon had another dilemma. Some of the women with disabilities had gathered and wanted to boycott the session. They saw it as hypocritical for members of the disabilities movement to put on a workshop that not everyone could attend. Others felt the content of the session was important enough to make the necessary sacrifices. The presenters compromised. They came down the stairs to meet those waiting in the lobby, in a show of solidarity. This ultimately was not satisfactory to all; the presenters went back upstairs to salvage their session and wrote a press release about the inaccessibility of the forum.

The rest of the women with disabilities remained in the lobby, by necessity or by choice. They were very angry about the position into which the disability delegation was put by the inept and illogical organization of the site. Planning disability-themed events in venues with no elevators, and on second and third floors, divided and compromised us. With this realization, we became very angry. Adrenalin pumping, we went outside the Great Hall and stood on the steps. They were like a stage looking onto a great courtyard where many people passed. This was far away from the small, approved and designated demonstration zone, but our anger seemed to remove this detail from our minds.

We began chanting, *"We want access now!"* over and over. People started to gather as we shouted that we were there because the workshop we wanted to attend was up all those stairs. Women from Africa gave passionate and animated impromptu speeches about our conditions at the forum and got us started in many choruses of "We Shall Overcome" that we changed to "We Want Access Now." Being in such a prominent place, we started to attract more people, including members of the various media. We were not motivated by trying to get the media's attention. Our action was purely a response fueled by the anger, frustration and disappointment that had come from our marginalization at this event. The media, however, were very interested in our spontaneous demonstration. During our chants, songs and speeches, we were filmed, recorded and photographed by media from all over the globe. After the controversial workshop had ended, most of the women who did attend the session came down and joined us. We decided to hold another "media event" the next day. We decided to call it a "media event" because we didn't want to use the vernacular of "protest" or "demonstration" — we were out of the designated zone for demonstrations. I spent the evening calling all the members of the media whom I had already met in China and as many women with disabilities as I could. I also had a meeting with a Canadian women's group — the National Action Committee on the Status of Women (NAC) — and I briefed them about our issues and the next day's events.

These efforts, as well as the efforts of so many other women with disabilities, went into making our second event as successful as we could have hoped. Jamala Albaidhani of the Yemen Society for Rehabilitation of the Physically Handicapped was at both events. She said: "I was extremely moved and impressed by the protest that the disabled women did yesterday, especially when we had the impression that, logistically, the place was going to be really easily accessible to disabled women. I was glad that there was this protest."

On the second day of the protest, the media came in very large numbers and really gave us a lot of attention and, surprisingly, respect. Judging from the newspaper articles and feedback about what was shown on TV, the media treated our struggle as a human rights issue rather than in the usual superficial manner of a human interest story. I haven't figured out if this is because the media was looking for a human rights infraction in China or whether real progress had been made in awareness. In any case, our faces, chants and interviews were beamed around the world. Many people saw us on the CBC news in Canada. There were reports from other countries that our demonstration was carried on CNN. Kathleen Guy of Trinidad said that images of our protest were seen in her country.

Other than our "media event," there were many people trying more diplomatic means to obtain better access for our delegation. Justine Kiwanuka, projects officer at the world headquarters for

Disabled Peoples' International, tried calling the China Organizing Committee and other officials. Many other women set up meetings with officials from the China Organizing Committee and their countries. But there was little to be done, as the changes that needed to be made should have been made months ago.

What is so frustrating is that women with disabilities were represented at all the preparatory meetings for this forum. We have made access an issue at every major international meeting that has been held in the recent past — from the Earth Summit to the Social Summit to the Conference on Population. It makes one wonder exactly what was learned by the United Nations' Decade of Disabled Persons (which ended in 1992) if the UN does not make its own meetings and documents accessible.

Undoubtedly, the late site change caused many problems, and perhaps the Chinese Organizing Committee didn't have the resources to figure out what accessibility really means. This might be true, in part, but the fact still remains that they had plenty of resources for information, such as the China Disabled Person's Federation, which put on workshops and gave us great support in the pre-conference symposium on women with disabilities. The organizing committee also had a lot of information from the delegates about their needs. China even had a wheelchair-user on its official government delegation. Zhang Haidi is a very famous writer, scholar, artist and businesswoman in China. She has written seven books (including her autobiographical novel, *Wheelchair Dream*) and has made regular television appearances. She is an authentic Chinese celebrity and was treated as such by the Chinese people when she visited our tent.

It is only common sense not to put workshops about women with disabilities on the top floors of buildings with no elevators. I feel that is a blatant sign of disrespect, not to mention totally illogical. I don't think that it was expected that so few, seemingly insignificant, women with disabilities would have had the power to alert the world to the disrespect that was shown to us. In fact, our protests, chants and lobbying were effective — our tent was moved to a site closer to the gates, on more even and stable ground.

Even though many of our workshops were cancelled or postponed, and even though we could not make our voices heard in all the workshops, we know our presence made an impact at the forum.

Just by being there, we made other delegates, the Organizing Committee, security and governments aware that we are here and want — no, demand — to be included. The fact that so many delegations included women with disabilities demonstrated that the women's movement really is trying to include us. I had so much support from the Canadian delegation — they really showed me, over and over, that they wanted me there and valued my voice.

Being valued like that really made all the struggles to be there worthwhile. The networking and sisterhood of the women in the disabilities tent made for strong motivation to get back on the bus and ride to the site from Beijing for two hours each day. Because of the conditions, much of the work that was to be accomplished by women with disabilities at the forum will have to be completed from a distance. We will have to go back home and write to each other to exchange ideas. Papers we were to present will have to be submitted to newsletters or journals. I hope that the women's movement will translate their support into action and publish our works.

The concept of "Beijing" did not, after all, find its realization, in the short time that all those women were gathered in one place. It is a continuum. There were years of preparation that went into that gathering and there are years of networking and follow-up still to come. My version of what happened at the NGO forum is not the definitive one — each and every delegate will have her own perspective and add something new.

In the end, I did get a brief opportunity to fulfill my obligation to the Canadian Research Institute for the Advancement of Women. I really wanted to go to the workshop called Grassroots Organizing for Action, which was sponsored by a U.S. group, the National Organization of Women. I was not surprised to find that the workshop was located on the fifth floor of a building and that, of course, there was no elevator. I stopped women in the stairwell and asked if they could send down the facilitator of the workshop to see if we could conduct it on a lower floor. By the time someone had come back down, I had found an empty room and obtained permission to use it. The facilitator agreed to the change and the workshop was moved. That really was grassroots organizing for action.

In a discussion on the street with a group of Chinese merchants, one man commented that this conference really was for the women who did not have emancipation or the personal freedoms to be there. I have to say that I totally agreed with him. That is why I will leave you with these words by Christine Kania from Uganda who speaks for so many of us when she says:

> *I knew Beijing was an NGO forum on women, and I knew I was a woman first and a disabled woman second. I came on a double ticket — first, as a woman to lobby for the rights of women, and, [second,] knowing that the disabled women are doubly disadvantaged. So I said: "Okay let me go there as a woman and a disabled woman and give my input the best way I know how." I hope that I created an impact and that I, together with other disabled women, created an impact on the women's movement, and also on the UN, that disability issues and disabled women's issues are also human rights issues. Our issues must also be highlighted and be given due importance. Even as we talk, we would be kidding ourselves if we thought that disability matters here, that disabled women matter here or had been given the same weight as the rest. I don't think so. One would be fooling oneself and be deceiving oneself and joking. And I thought if I came here, if we came here — if I shouted and if other women shouted and we all shouted together — it might make a bigger impact, a little more than if one talked individually or than if we kept ourselves away.*

> *I have made my contribution. I have given my experiences of my disabled organization back home, and the conditions of disabled women back home socially, economically, and the limitations we have in term terms of education, financially and culturally. I have made people aware of what we go through. I have made an appeal ... I can go back and be used and use what I've seen here to improve the conditions of those women and bring them into the mainstream disability movement.*

Diane Driedger &
E. Catherine Boldt

Conclusions

The connections that have been developed by the women in this book are very strong and valuable. We have crossed many barriers to be able to work so well with one another. Despite our differences, we are united by one common denominator — we are women with disabilities. We may live in different climates, have different diets and look different from one another, but we all know what it is like to live as a woman with a disability. There is no culture in the world that accepts and fully integrates us. We have all had to struggle to have our voices heard in society, the workplace, academia, our communities and even our own homes. Women with disabilities throughout the world are united by these facts.

We are also increasingly becoming involved with the political process. With very few resources, we are involved — from local committees and governments all the way to lobbying the United Nations (UN). We have been present at all recent UN conferences and preparations. We are demanding to be included and consulted on any UN convention and declarations, whether it is a convention against sex trafficking or the rights of the child. We are insisting that governments and communities recognize that what affects the life of any other woman also affects us, sometimes even more intensely.

Because of all that we have in common, we have quickly developed close relationships with each other whenever we have come together. We have also spent time visiting each other's communities and developing our relationships even further. This time spent in exchange is far more valuable than the brief and superficial information that can be exchanged at a conference. We have been in each others' homes and have developed a complete picture of each others' lives. We have had real personal impact on one another. The networks we have built in this way give us strength and ideas to take home to our own communities.

We have all been involved in identifying and organizing women with disabilities in our own communities. Encouraging women to leave their homes is a great victory. This is a real struggle for many of us, but it is the first step towards becoming a viable force. The articles in this book indicate that we have also had to educate and inform the larger disabilities communities of our own unique issues as women. Sometimes, the men in our greater disability movement have been supportive, and sometimes they have been tentative in offering support.

We have also gone beyond our boundaries and reached out to the women's community and educated them about our particular perspective. Women with disabilities have found that the educational process takes a long time, and that we have to continue to offer up our voices to change perceptions within the women's movement. We are now represented on many women's coalitions all over the world, but our work within feminist communities and other progressive social movements has been long and hard. Often, we go forward in educating a particular community and then fall back, disappointed by their inability or unwillingness to truly include us. Changing these attitudes is an ongoing process, as was demonstrated at the inaccessible Beijing conference. But, as we also demonstrated in Beijing, we are a strong and vocal segment of the women's community. There is no going back — our concerns about access are here to stay.

We have gone to the international development community with our message that disability rights are human rights, and we have shown that disability is indeed a development issue. There has been a tendency for non-governmental organizations (NGOs) all over the world to perceive disability as a medical charity issue, not a human rights concern. Only a few years ago, the women's community was told by governments and the international community that women's rights were not necessarily human rights. We assert that the rights of people with disabilities are human rights issues as well; we have been asserting this for over 15 years.

The Council of Canadians with Disabilities (CCD), and many of CCD's partners, continue to establish links with governmental, non-governmental and UN agencies to further the societal integration of women with disabilities. Indeed, we, as women with disabilities, will continue working together for our emancipation from limiting attitudes and environments — and we will continue to do so across all the world's borders.

Contributors' Notes

Francine Arsenault has been involved in the disability rights movement in Canada since the early 1980s. Francine has multiple disabilities, but reports that she is still mobile and energetic! A past chair of the Council of Canadians with Disabilities, she is currently chair of the International Centre for the Advancement of Community Based Rehabilitation. She has travelled widely, facilitating Community Based Rehabilitation workshops in a number of countries and has worked with United Nations agencies as a disabilities consultant. Francine lectures at Queen's University. She, and her husband and their three children live in a log home they built themselves in Perth Road Village, Ontario, Canada.

Keny Avilés was born in El Salvador in October 1973. One of five children, she had polio as a very young child. She is presently majoring in Law at the University of El Salvador. She has also done some research on violence against women. Keny has been an active participant in the women's movement for several years, which is unusual for a young woman in El Salvador. Keny enjoys writing poetry.

Monica J. Bartley is a director of the Administrative Statistics Division of the Statistical Institute of Jamaica. Monica has been involved with disability work on a voluntary basis since 1975. She served as chairperson of the Combined Disabilities Association (CDA) from 1988-90 and as chairperson of the Disabled Peoples' International (DPI) North America & Caribbean Region from 1992-94. She currently is the honorary secretary of DPI as well as a member of: the National Advisory Board, Committee for Students with Disabilities (University of the West Indies); Diversified Economic Enterprise for Disabled Self-help Industries Ltd.; CDA and the CDA Women's Group; and the Mona Rehabilitation Centre Old Girls Association.

E. Catherine Boldt was told in school that she could barely read but had a nice personality! She is a contributing author to a published book and has had many other articles published. A member of the Council of Canadians with Disabilities International Committee and a board member of the Canadian Research Insitiute for the Advancement of Women, she is a disabilities activist and consultant. In her spare time, she enjoys water sports, singing and writing poetry.

Pat Danforth has over 20 years experience in human rights issues, including advocacy organizations for persons with disabilities and women's organizations. She has worked with the Saskatchewan Human Rights Commission since 1985 in both investigations and programmes. Pat is a founding member of Council of Canadians with Disabilities and Dis-Abled Women's Network Canada. She serves as a volunteer with a variety of organizations. She is a single parent and collects sand (yes, sand) from everywhere. She is always asking folks that travel to bring back sand for her ... She writes when she feels life gets too hard to manage.

Diane Driedger has authored two books: a chapbook of poetry entitled *Darkness is a Marshmallow* (Moonprint, 1994) and *The Last Civil Rights Movement: Disabled Peoples' International* (Hurst and St. Martin's, 1989). She has also co-edited two books: *Imprinting Our Image: An International Anthology by Women with Disabilities* (gynergy books, 1992) and *Across Borders: Women with Disabilities Working Together* (gynergy books, 1996). Diane has worked in the disability movement for many years and has also served on the board of the Canadian Research Institute for the Advancement of Women, where she was chair of the Global Feminisms Committee. She currently lives in Winnipeg, Manitoba, Canada.

Irene Feika's favourite pastime is writing poetry and prose — "I believe that poetry is the voice of our souls." *Across Borders: Women with Disabilities Working Together* (gynergy books, 1996) is her first co-editing project. Irene lives in Edmonton, Alberta, Canada.

Eileen Girón Batres says, "I am pleased to collaborate with so many women with disabilities as a writer and co-editor of *Across Borders: Women with Disabilities Working Together* [gynergy books, 1996]. May it inspire disabled women everywhere to organize." She lives in San Salvador, El Salvador.

Michele Green holds a PhD in British History and continues her academic work as an independent scholar in Toronto, Canada. She also write articles and facilitate workshops on disability issues for various charitable and service organizations. Her passion is riding; she rides at the Community Association for Riding for the Disabled. Michele says, "I am pleased that some of my poems have been published, whether in *Green's Magazine* or *Transitions* or local newsletters. And I am delighted to be a part of this project."

Kathleen Guy is co-founder and coordinator of the Disabled Women's Network Trinidad and Tobago. She has worked as a nurse and as a businesswoman. She was a member of one of the first women's organizations in Trinidad and Tobago, the Coterie of Social Workers. Kathleen is blind.

Nuggehalli Sitaram Hema is a founder-trustee of the Association of the Physically Handicapped (APH), established in 1959, at Bangalore, India. Currently, she is the president of APH. Living with a disability since the age of four, Hema views her physical condition as a tool in her work with other persons. She uses her emotional strengths to inspire and motivate others. "My true awards are not those that have been handed to me on stage, but the work that the organization has done and the changes it has brought in the lives of people."

Judy Heumann is presently assistant secretary of education for the Office of Special Education and Rehabilitation Services (OSERS), where she and her staff of 350 people oversee programming, administration and research with a budget of 5.5 billion dollars. These funds are directed at the 49 million disabled citizens of the Unites States. Since her appointment in 1993, Judy has worked to make OSERS' programmes more accessible to disabled individuals from minority and culturally diverse backgrounds. Judy has been involved as a disability activist both nationally and internationally and has become a de facto ambassador for the disabled community in the United States. Most recently, she was appointed a member of the U.S. delegation to the Fourth World Conference on Women, in Beijing, China, by President Clinton. Judy now lives in Washington, D.C. with her husband, Jorge Pineda.

Joyce Joseph, of Trinidad and Tobago, runs a dressmaking business. She is active in Disabled Peoples' International Trinidad and Tobago, the self-help organization of disabled persons. She is also very active in church work.

K-Lynn says, "Poetry became a way of coping with several tragedies that occurred seven years ago. Today, creative writing is a fundamental aspect of my life. Although enjoyment and spontaneity remain the priorities, I use poetry as a teaching tool for others to increase their awareness of disability and the issues." She lives in Canada.

Justine Kiwanuka was born in Uganda and lived in Kenya for five years before coming to Canada in 1988. Currently working with Disabled

Peoples' International (DPI), she is responsible for issues of women with disabilities in DPI. She has had an opportunity to travel to Europe, Asia and Africa as part of her work and has attended several United Nations conferences, including the first International Symposium on Women with Disabilities and the Fourth World Conference on Women, both held recently in Beijing, China.

Lizzie (Mamvura) Langshaw was born in 1956 to a peasant farmer in the small town of Marondera, Zimbabwe. She is the only child in the family. She became disabled at the age of two years and says her disability is very challenging and very inspiring at times. She is coordinating the National Council of Disabled Persons of Zimbabwe Women's Group Development Programme and enjoys working with women which is very challenging and sometimes requires a lot of patience. She is the mother of two boys, and likes to spend her weekends cooking for her family.

Cathy Lysack is a doctoral student in Community Health Sciences at the University of Manitoba in Winnipeg, Canada. Cathy has spent time in rural Indonesia studying community-based disability projects, and the barriers to women's voluntarism in these projects. At present, Cathy is interested in the nature and scope of the disability rights movement in different cultures in the developing world. She gratefully acknowledges the assistance of both Disabled Peoples' International in her research, and the National Health Research Development Programme for its PhD Fellowship support.

Maritza Melara Castillo was born in 1968 in El Salvador, the youngest in the family. She says, "When I was five years old, I stopped running in the garden, because I got polio, but this was not a major problem since I learned to enjoy playing games with my peers. When I finished high school I went to the university to study Business Administration. I found many problems and barriers on my way, but I was able to overcome them. Now I have a lot of work, but what I enjoy the most is having so many friends and being a volunteer in ACOGIPRI [Asociación Cooperativa del Grupo Independiente Pro Rehabilitación Integral]."

Mary Mitchell was born in the parish of St. Catherine, Jamaica. She enjoys working with organizations of persons with disabilities. She is a former chairperson of the Combined Disabilities Association of Jamaica, West Indies. She is visually impaired as a result of an accident.

Shingirai Pensado was born in Zimbabwe on June 22, 1963. In 1982, she became ill and has used a wheelchair since 1985. Although she wrote her 'O' levels and passed in English, Shona, Commerce and Geography as well as doing some computer work in Lotus 123 and Word Perfect, she is single and unemployed. She says, "I sometimes forget that I am disabled until I am unable to do something — that is when my life becomes a burden. I love writing, acting, watching movies and public relations."

Ruth Rodriguez was born in San Salvador, El Salvador in 1964. She became disabled at 23; she was working full time and going to the university when she had a stroke. She received speech therapy in order to be able to speak again. She was very dependent on her family, especially her mother, to do everything. Ruth heard about the Asociación Cooperativa del Grupo Independiente Pro Rehabilitación Integral women's programme and started to attend the meetings. Little by little, she got involved to the point that she became the coordinator of the programme. She has turned into a very independent woman.

Donna M. Sinclair says, "I lead a quiet life with my mother, sister, and grandmother in Spanish Town, the capital of St. Catherine in Jamaica. I have been writing poems since the early 1980s. I am physically disabled and use a wheelchair. I am not married. My hobbies are reading, crocheting and making book-markers."

Lorraine Thomas is a 23-year-old, hearing-impaired woman from the Republic of Trinidad and Tobago. She is a graduate of English Literature and is co-editor of a local disability magazine called *Trinidad and Tobago DPI Advocate*. Lorraine works as assistant to the director of Health Education Division, Ministry of Health. She started writing poetry in high school. Lorraine hopes to publish a collection of writings some day and intends to do her Masters in Mass Communications "soon."

Eudalie Wickham is an active member of the National Organization of the Disabled (BARNOD) and the disability movement in Barbados. She is visually impaired, loves writing, reading and firmly believes in God. She has one daughter.

Selected Bibliography

Abernethy, V. "The world's women: Fighting a battle, losing the war." *Journal of Women's Health* 2, 1 (1993). pp. 7-16.

Asia Partnership for Human Development. *Awake: Asian women and the struggle for justice.* Sydney, Australia: Asia Partnership for Human Development, 1985.

Boylan, Esther. *Women and Disability.* London, England and New Jersey, USA: Zed Books, 1991.

Canadian Disability Rights Council and DisAbled Women's Network Canada. *Four Discussion Papers on New Reproductive Technologies.* Winnipeg, Canada: CDRC and DAWN, 1990.

Chermak, G. "A global perspective on disability: A review of efforts to increase access and advance social integration for disabled persons." *International Disability Studies* 12, (1990). pp. 123-7.

Cocks, E. "Encouraging a paradigm shift in services for people with disabilities." *Social Research and Development*, Monograph No. 9. Perth, Australia: Centre for the Development of Human Resources, Edith Cowan University, 1994.

Cottone, L., and R. Cottone. "Women and disabilities: On the paradox of empowerment and the need for a trans-systemic and feminist perspective." *Journal of Applied Rehabilitation Counselling* 23, 4 (1992). pp. 20-5.

Deegan, M., and N. Brooks. *Women and disability: The double handicap.* New Brunswick, NJ, USA: Transaction Books, 1985.

Driedger, Diane. *The Last Civil Rights Movement: Disabled Peoples' International.* London, England and New York, USA: C. Hurst & Co. and St. Martin's Press, 1989.

Driedger, Diane (ed.). *Disabled People in International Development.* Winnipeg, Canada: Coalition of Provincial Organizations of the Handicapped, 1991.

Driedger, Diane. "Discovering Disabled Women's History," in *The More We Get Together: Women and Disability.* Houston Stewart, Beth Percival and Elizabeth R. Epperley (eds.). Charlottetown, Canada: gynergy books, 1992. pp. 81-93.

Driedger, Diane and April D'Aubin. "Discarding the Shroud of Silence: An International Perspective on Violence, Women and Disability." *Canadian Woman Studies* 12 (Fall 1991). pp. 81-3.

Driedger, Diane and April D'Aubin. "Literacy for Whom? Women with Disabilities Marginalized." *Women's Education des femmes* 8 (Winter 1991). pp. 6-10.

Doucette, Joanne. "Redefining Difference: Disabled Lesbians Resist," in *Lesbians in Canada.* Sharon Dale Stone (ed.). Toronto, Canada: Between the Lines, 1990. pp. 61-72.

Dueck, Susan Gray. "Stepping Stones to the Land of the Living." *Women's Education des femmes* 9 (Spring 1992). pp. 13-5.

French, S. "Researching disability: The way forward." *Disability and Rehabilitation* 14, 4 (1992). pp. 183-6.

Fricke, Yutta. "International Year for Literacy: Education for All?" *Vox Nostra* 1 (1990). pp. 6-7.

Fuller, T., J. Edwards, S. Sermsri and S. Vorakitphokatorn. "Gender and health: Some Asian evidence." *Journal of Health and Social Behavior* 34 (1993). pp. 252-71.

Grant, J. "One hundred and fifty million disabled children and growing." *One-in-Ten* 13 (1994). pp. 1-8.

ILO, UNESCO and WHO. "Community-based rehabilitation (CBR) for and with people with disabilities." Joint Position Paper. Geneva: ILO, UNESCO and WHO, 1994.

Koblinsky, M., J. Timyan and J. Gay. *The health of women: A global perspective.* Boulder, CO, USA: Westview Press, 1993.

Lee, M., J. Hezekiah and D. Watters. "Rural women and power in Pakistan." *Health Care for Women International* 16 (1995). pp. 125-33.

Lysack, C. "Community participation and community-based rehabilitation: An Indonesian case study." *Occupational Therapy International* 2, 3 (1995). pp. 149-65.

Lysack, C., and L. Krefting. "Community based rehabiltiation cadres and their motivation for volunteerism." *International Journal of Rehabilitation Research* 16 (1993). pp. 133-41.

Lysack, C., and L. Krefting. "The myths of volunteerism and the women who make community based rehabilitation work." *CBR News* 17 (London, England: May-August, 1994). p. 5.

MacCormack, C. "Health and the social power of women." *Social Science and Medicine* 26 (1988). pp. 677-83.

Masuda, Shirley with Jillian Ridington. *Meeting Our Needs: Access Manual for Transition Houses.* Winnipeg, Canada: DisAbled Women's Network Canada, 1990.

McPherson, Cathy. *Responding to the Abuse of People with Disabilities.* Toronto, Canada: Advocacy Resource Centre for the Handicapped, 1990.

Morris, J. "Feminism and disability." *Feminist Review* 43 (Spring, 1993). pp. 57-70.

Parpart, J. "Who is the 'other'?: A postmodern feminist critique of women and development theory and practice." *Development and Change* 24 (1993). pp. 439-64.

Petersen, A. "Community development in health promotion: Empowerment or regulation?" *Australian Journal of Public Health* 18, 2 (1994). pp. 213-7.

Racino, J., and J. Heumann. "Independent living and community life." *Aging and disabilities* 16, 1 (1992). pp. 43-7.

Rajah, Zohra. "Thoughts on Women and Disability." *Vox Nostra* 2 (1989). p. 10.

Ridington, Jillian. *Beating the "Odds": Violence and Women with Disabilities.* Vancouver, Canada: DAWN Canada, 1989.

Rodriguez, Kenwyn. *Equalization of Opportunities: Proceedings of the 3rd World Congress of Disabled Peoples' International, Vancouver, Canada, April 21-26, 1994.* Winnipeg, Canada: DPI, 1994.

The Roeher Institute. *Social Well Being: A Paradigm for Reform*. Toronto, Canada: The Roeher Institute, 1993.

Shah, Dr. Fatima. "The Blind Woman and Her Family and Participation in the Community (Rural)," in *Women, Development and Disability*. Ann Gajerski-Cauley (ed.). Winnipeg, Canada: Coalition of Provincial Organizations of the Handicapped, 1989. p. 20.

Stackhouse, J. "Why health is a motherhood issue." *The Globe and Mail* (Toronto, Canada: February 8, 1994). p. A13.

Stehlik, D. "Untying the knot: A socialist-feminist analysis of the social construction of care." *Social Research and Development, Monograph No. 7*. Perth, Australia: Centre for the Development of Human Resources, Edith Cowan University, 1993.

Stuart, Meryn and Glynis Ellerington. "Unequal Access: Disabled Women's Exclusion from the Mainstream Women's Movement." *Women and Environments* 12 (Spring 1990). pp. 16-9.

Symke, P. *Women and Health*. London, England: Zed Books, 1991.

United Nations. "Seminar on Disabled Women: Draft Report, August 20-24, 1990." Vienna: UN, 1990.

Wheeler, Kelly and Gem Wirszilas (eds.). *Visions of Flight: A journey of positive thought by and about women with disabilities*. Surrey, BC, Canada: self-published, 1991.

WHO *Disability Prevention and Rehabilitation: Report of the WHO Expert, Technical Report Series No. 668*. Geneva: WHO, 1981.

Index

Combined Disabilities Association (CDA) 27, 30, 32-34, 43-44
Combined Disabilities Association Women's Group (CDA Women's Group) 26-36
community based rehabilitation (CBR) 101, 112-124, 133
Consulting Committee on the Status of Women with Disabilities (CCSWD) 15
Costa Rica 17, 54, 57
See also Fifth Multidisciplinary Women's Congress
Council of Canadians with Disabilities (CCD) 7-9, 12-15, 25, 33, 40-41, 46, 58, 75-78, 80-81, 83, 117, 120, 123, 132, 141, 143, 146, 150, 163
International Committee 9, 76

Disability International USA (DI USA) 12
Disabled in Action (DIA) 88-89
Disabled Peoples' International (DPI) 8-9, 12-13, 17-19, 21, 28-29, 32, 40, 52, 131, 133, 157
Women and Development seminar 28-29
Disabled Peoples' International Trinadad and Tobago (DPI T&T) 71-81
Disabled Women's International (DWI) 18
DisAbled Women's Network Canada (DAWN Canada) 15-17, 19, 25, 77
Disabled Women's Network of Trinidad and Tobago (DAWN T&T) 16, 22, 60, 71-81, 85-86
educational upgrading programme 79
health maintenance training programme 16, 79
poetry workshop 60-63, 78
Diversified Economic Enterprise for Disabled Self-help (DEEDS) Industries 46
Dominica 17, 28, 43

education and training 7-10, 16, 19-22, 26, 29-30, 32-36, 40-43, 45-46, 52-55, 57, 63, 67, 73, 75-79, 81-82, 87-89, 101-103, 110-111, 114-115, 118, 120, 123, 132-133, 135, 141-143, 149
El Salvador 8-9, 12, 17, 37, 49, 51-59, 65, 132, 151
See also ACOGIPRI, MUJERES '94, Sixth Latin America and Carribean Feminist Meeting
employment 8, 10, 15-17, 19-22, 26-27, 30, 34-36, 45-46, 52-53, 67, 72-74, 82, 87-88, 90, 92, 95-96, 99, 101-103, 110-111, 114, 118, 120
empowerment 44, 54, 56, 58, 79, 81, 110, 118, 121-124, 149
England 24, 34, 125, 151
Ethiopia 151

Fifth Multidisciplinary Women's Congress 57
Finland 151
Fourth World Conference on Women 8, 19, 31, 36, 39, 58, 67, 93, 97-98, 111, 135, 149, 150-160
Chinese Organizing Committee 153, 157-159

Germany 92
Global Fund for Women 79
Grenada 132
Guatemala 39, 54, 151
See also CAB, WK Kellogg Foundation

housing 14, 19, 26-27, 35, 84, 89, 91, 104, 121

Immigrant Access Service 146
Independent Living Centre of Trinidad and Tobago (ILC T&T) 75-78, 85
Independent Living Resource Centre (ILRC) 84, 146
India 98-110, 125, 132, 134
See also CBR, APH

Best of gynergy books

Each Small Step: Breaking the Chains of Abuse and Addiction, *Marilyn MacKinnon (ed.).* This groundbreaking anthology contains narratives by women recovering from the traumas of childhood sexual abuse and alcohol and chemical dependency. ISBN 0-921881-17-7 $10.95

Imprinting Our Image: An International Anthology by Women with Disabilities, *Diane Driedger, Susan Gray (eds.).* "In this global tour de force, 30 writers from 17 countries provide dramatic insight into a wide range of issues germane to both the women's and the disability rights movements." *Disabled Peoples' International*

"This book is enlightening and offers an opportunity to gain greater insight into the struggles of disabled women." *Canadian Journal of Occupational Therapy* ISBN 0-921881-22-3 $12.95

Invisible: Issues in Women's Occupational Health/La Santé des travailleuses, *Karen Messing, Barbara Neis, Lucie Dumais (eds.).* In *Invisible*, 18 respected researchers shed light on assumptions about women and work. By observing diverse occupations, the authors describe hidden hazards, reveal gender biases in research and explain delays in recognition of women's occupational health problems. ISBN 0-921881-37-1 $21.95

Patient No More: The Politics of Breast Cancer, *Sharon Batt.* "A spectacular book … carefully researched and thoroughly engrossing … As exciting to read as a Grisham thriller, it demonstrates that reality is more compelling than fiction." *Bloomsbury Review*

Winner of the *1995 Laura Jamieson Award* for best feminist non-fiction book, awarded by the Canadian Research Institute for the Advancement of Women (CRIAW). ISBN 0-921881-30-4 $19.95/$16.95 U.S.

gynergy books titles are available at quality bookstores. Ask for our titles at your favourite local bookstore. Individual, prepaid orders may be sent to: gynergy books, P.O. Box 2023, Charlottetown, Prince Edward Island, Canada, C1A 7N7. Please add postage and handling ($3 for the first book and 75 cents for each additional book) to your order. Canadian residents add 7% GST to the total amount. GST registration number R104383120. Prices are subject to change without notice.